I0540292

This book "bee"-longs to:

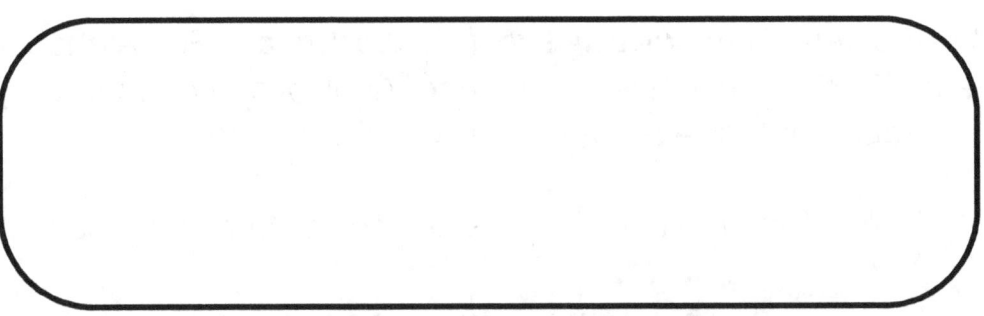

© 2024 Tuttle N Friends media LLC

© 2024 Tuttle N Friends Media LLC

Beezus Bee's Handwriting Practice Workbook! Fun Alphabet Letter Tracing Worksheets with Pencil Control and ABC Coloring Pages for Kids Ages 3-5 in Preschool and Kindergarten.

For More Information about us, please visit our website at:

tuttlenfriendsmedia.com

We would love to hear from you!

Scan the bar code below to contact us:

© 2024 Tuttle N Friends media LLC

Parents:

This book follows and "Edu-tainment" model of teaching. Edutainment is a blend of the words "education" and "entertainment." It refers to content designed to both educate and entertain, aiming to make learning more enjoyable and engaging. This approach leverages entertainment elements such as storytelling, humor, multimedia, and interactive activities to present educational material, enhancing the learning experience and often making it more effective.

Practicing tracing lines is a great way for your child to develop the fine motor skills needed for writing
Here's a step-by-step guide to help your child improve their hand control before they start learning the alphabet.

1. Begin with simple, straight lines: vertical, horizontal, and diagonal.

2. Progress to curved lines, circles, zigzags, and wavy lines.

3. Once your child is comfortable with tracing lines, introduce letters by using the alphabet tracing worksheets.

4. Set aside a few minutes each day for tracing practice.

By following these steps, you'll help your child build the foundational skills needed for writing the alphabet.

Happy tracing!

Scan here to download additional free practice sheets: →
Password: Beezus

tuttlenfriendsmedia.com

© 2024 Tuttle N Friends media LLC

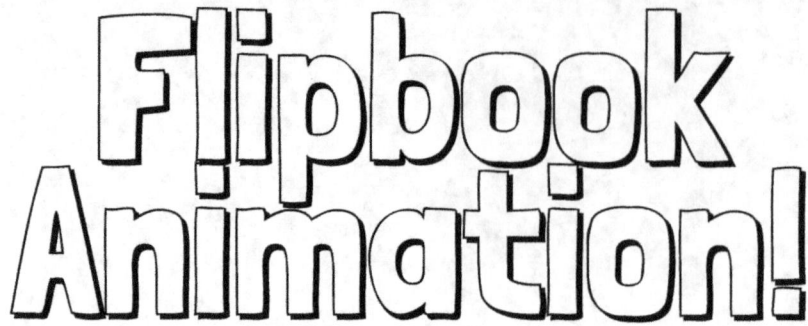

Flipbook Animation!

Watch Beezus Bee clap for your child when they finish all of the practice sheets!

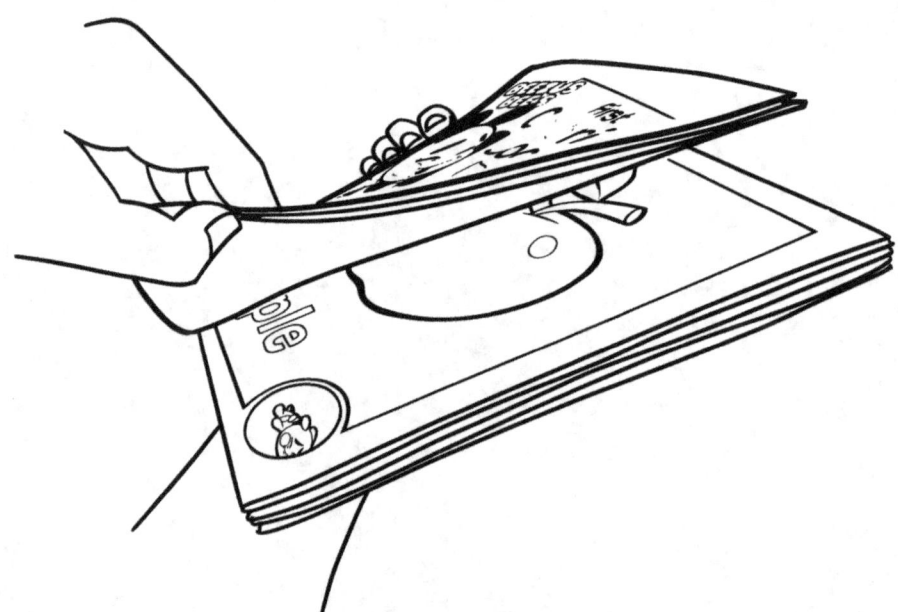

To use the flipbook, simply hold the book in one hand and use your thumb or fingers to flip through the pages quickly, creating the illusion of life as the images change from one page to the next. Adjusting the speed of your flips can control the speed of the animation. Start from the last page of the book and let the pages fall, making your way towards the front.

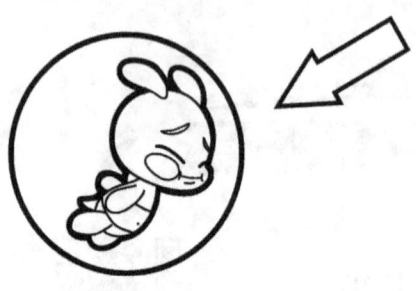

Ok! Let's Get Started!

© 2024 Tuttle N Friends media LLC

Can you trace these paths?

BEEZUS BEE'S *Letter Tracing* ~~Coloring~~ *Worksheets*

© 2024 Tuttle N Friends media LLC

Can you trace these paths?

BEEZUS BEE'S Letter Tracing Coloring Worksheets

© 2024 Tuttle N Friends media LLC

Can you help Pauly Penguin get to his fish ?

BEEZUS BEE'S Letter Tracing Coloring Worksheets

© 2024 Tuttle N Friends media LLC

Can you help the Prince find the Princess?

Dragon

BEEZUS BEE'S Letter Tracing Coloring Worksheets

© 2024 Tuttle N Friends media LLC

Can you help the monkey find the banana?

tuttlenfriendsmedia.com   BEEZUS BEE'S Letter Tracing Coloring Worksheets   © 2024 Tuttle N Friends media LLC

Can you help....

Ok, I might have gotten carried away a little bit.

Answer: Apple

BEEZUS BEE'S Letter Tracing Coloring Worksheets

© 2024 Tuttle N Friends media LLC

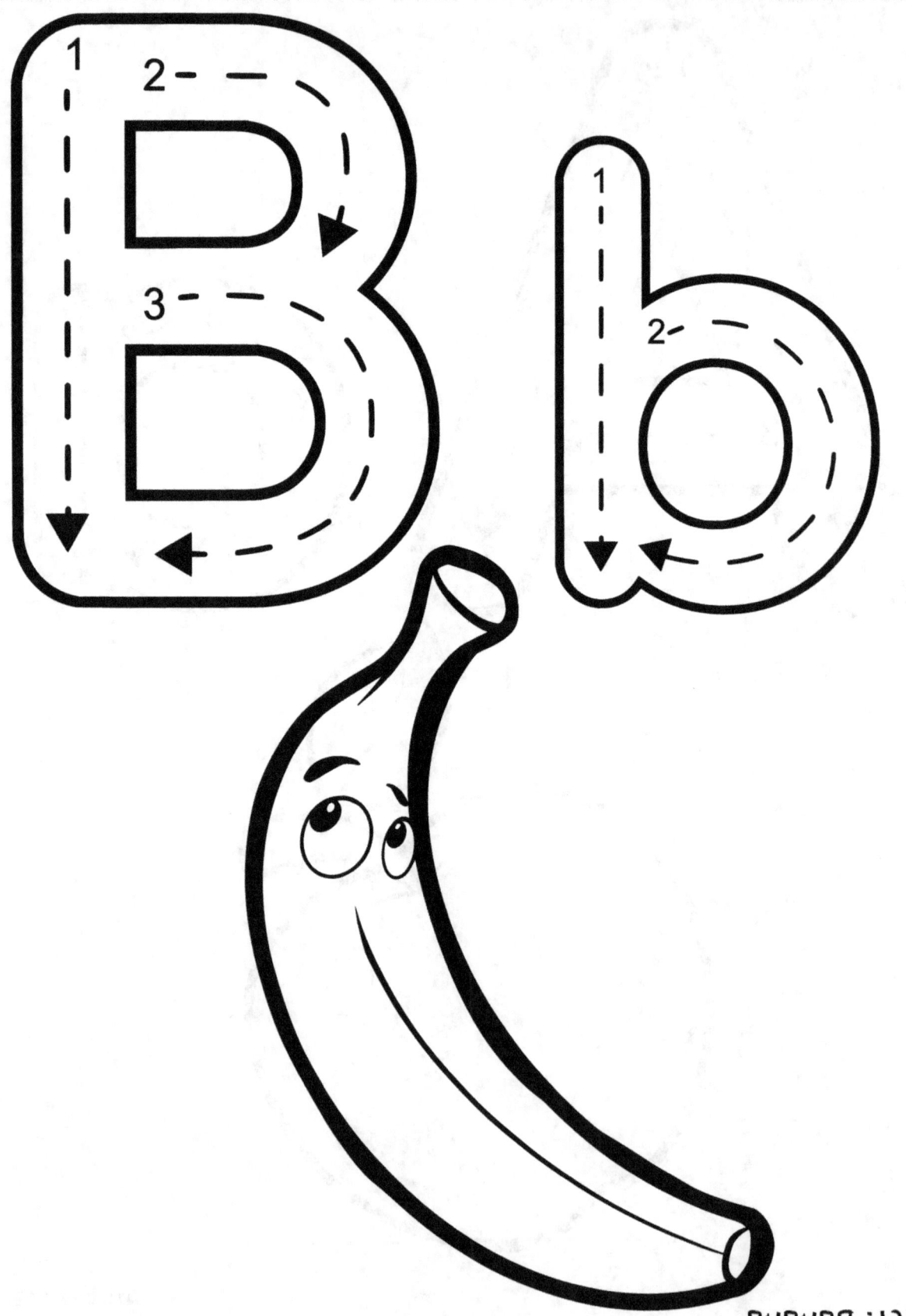

Answer: Banana

What fruit or vegetable starts with the letter..?

Answer: Cantaloupe

BEEZUS BEE'S Letter Tracing Coloring Worksheets

© 2024 Tuttle N Friends media LLC

Answer: Daikon Radish

© 2024 Tuttle N Friends media LLC

What fruit or vegetable starts with the letter..?

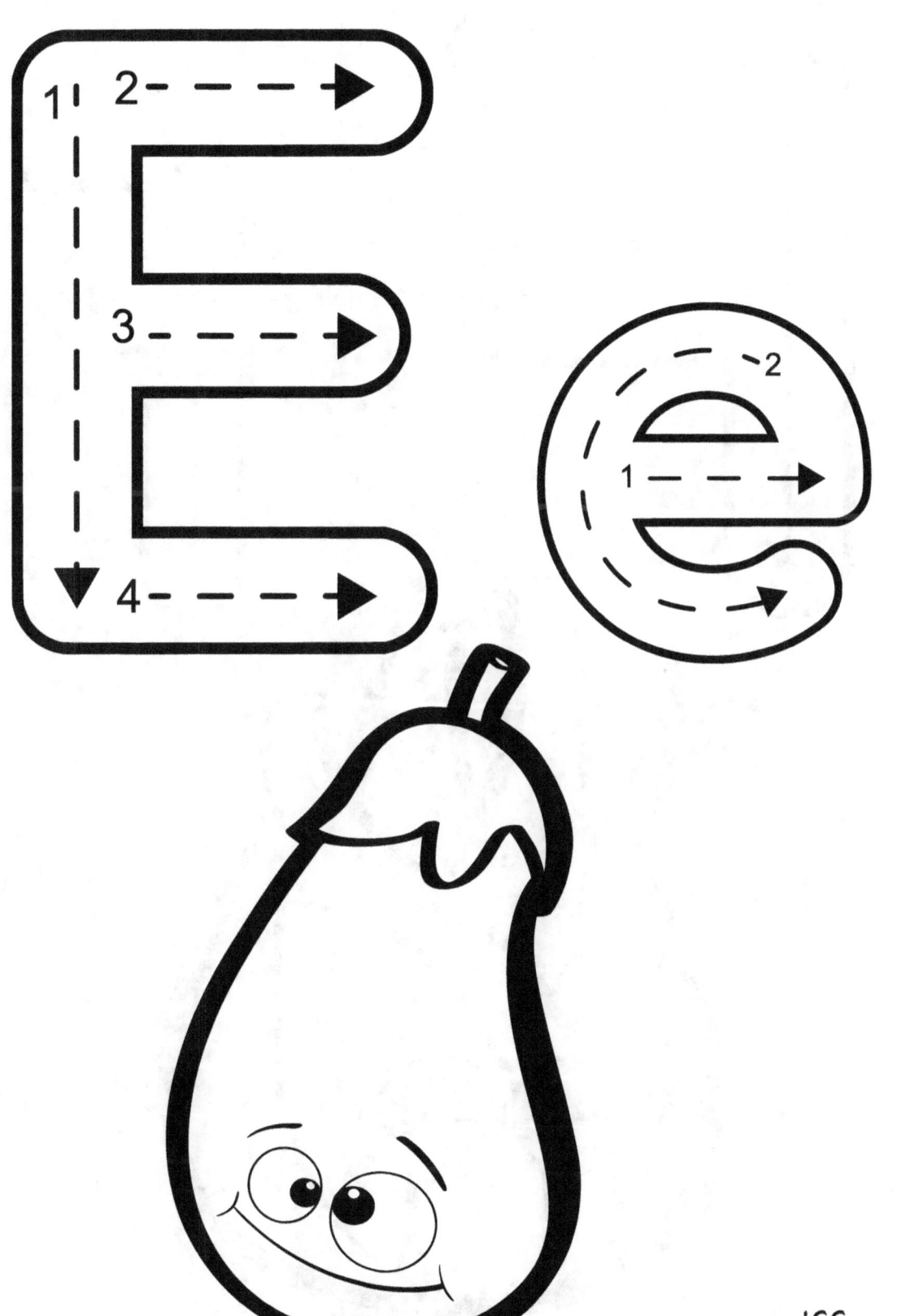

Answer: Eggplant

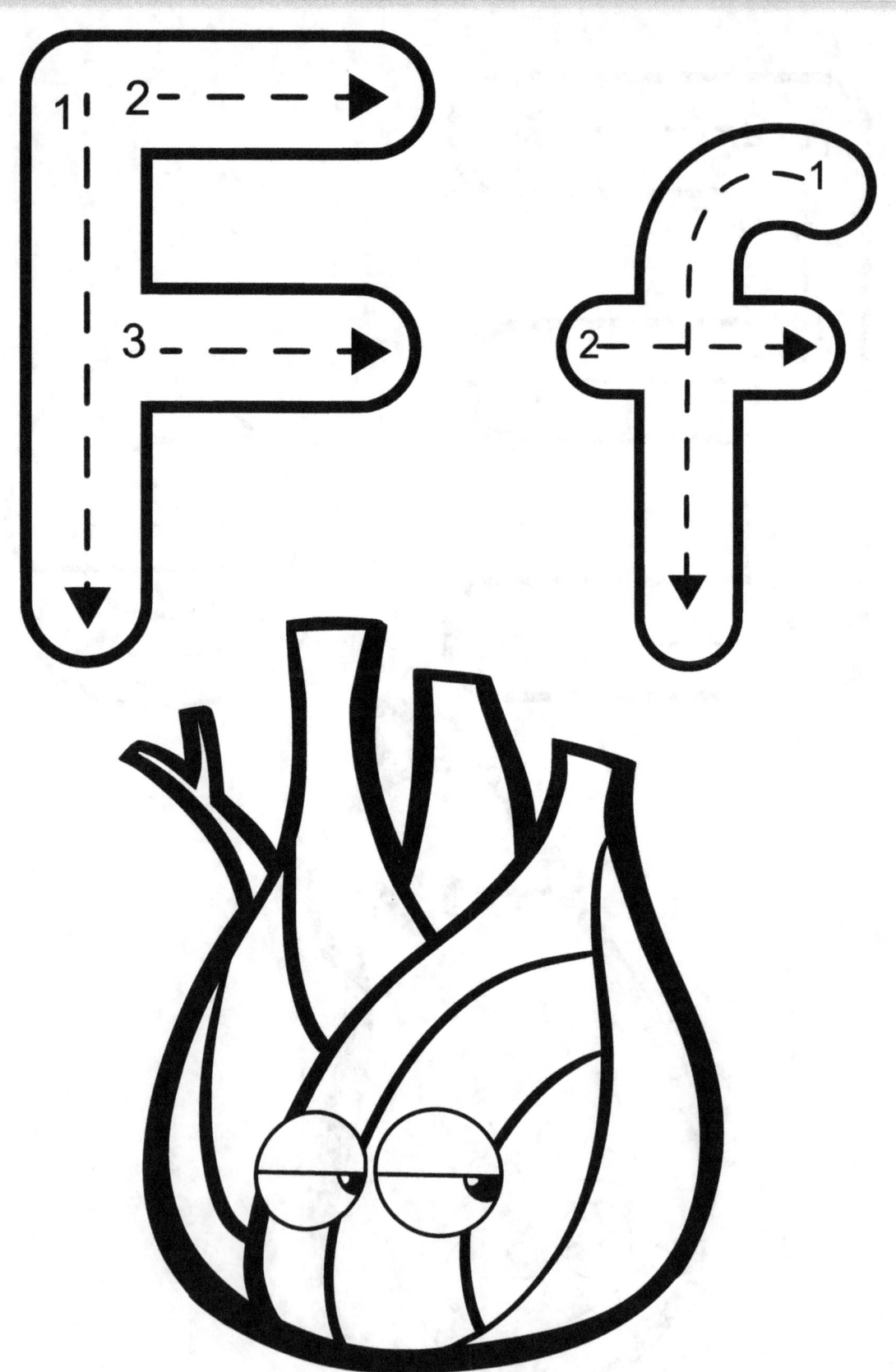

Answer: Fennel

What fruit or vegetable starts with the letter..?

Answer: Garlic

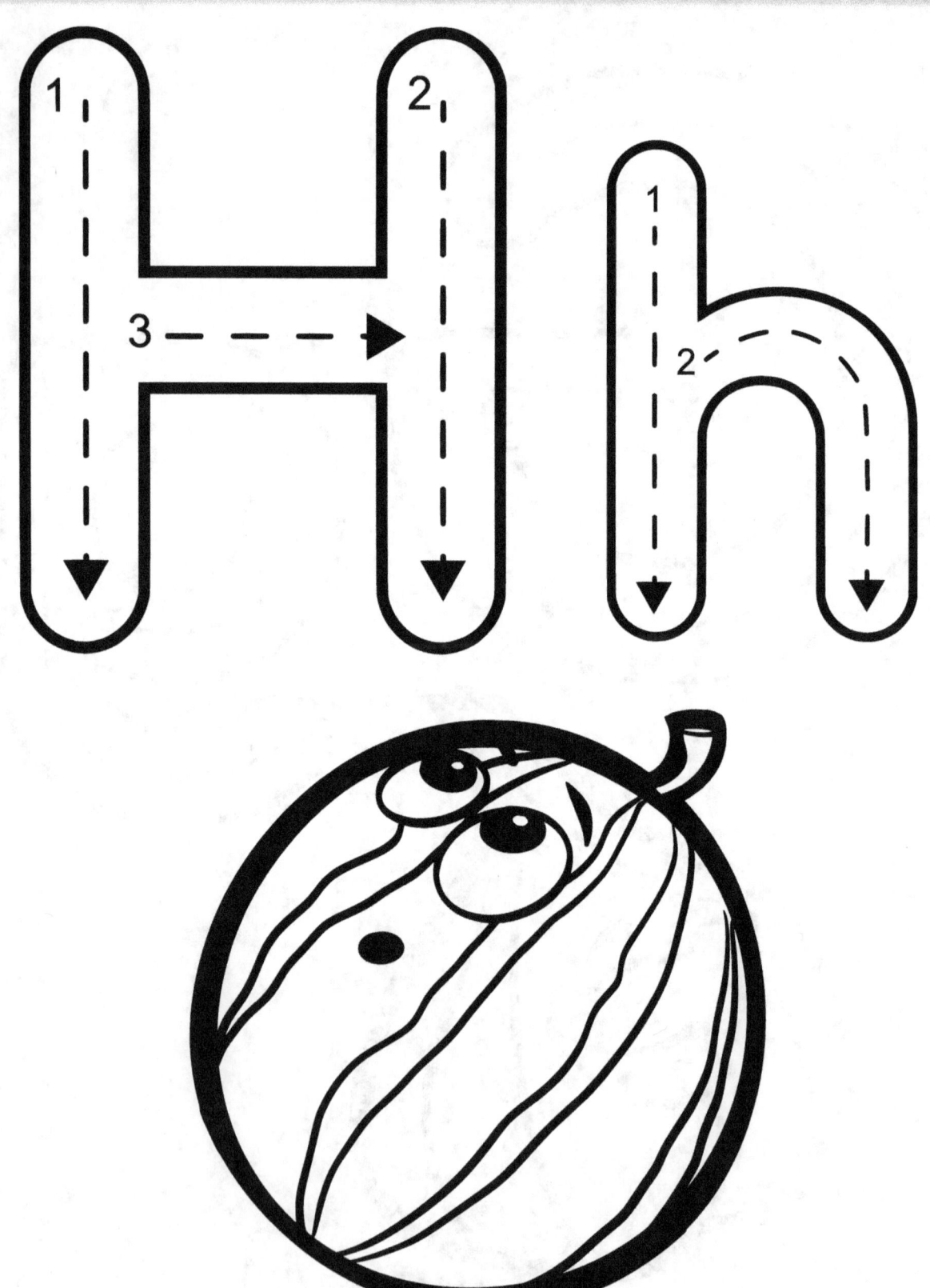

Answer: Honeydew Melon

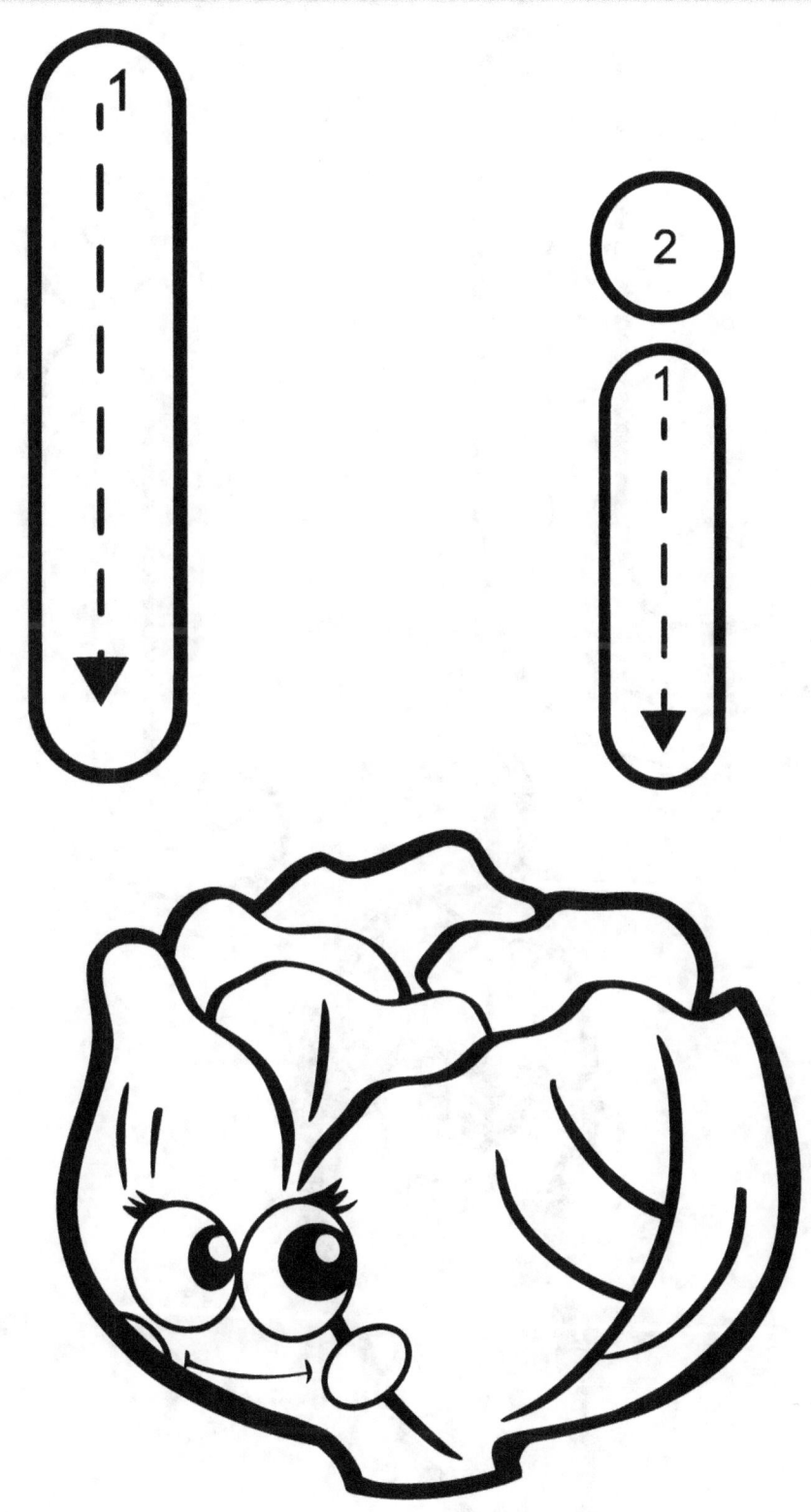

Answer: Iceberg lettuce

Answer: Jalapeno Pepper

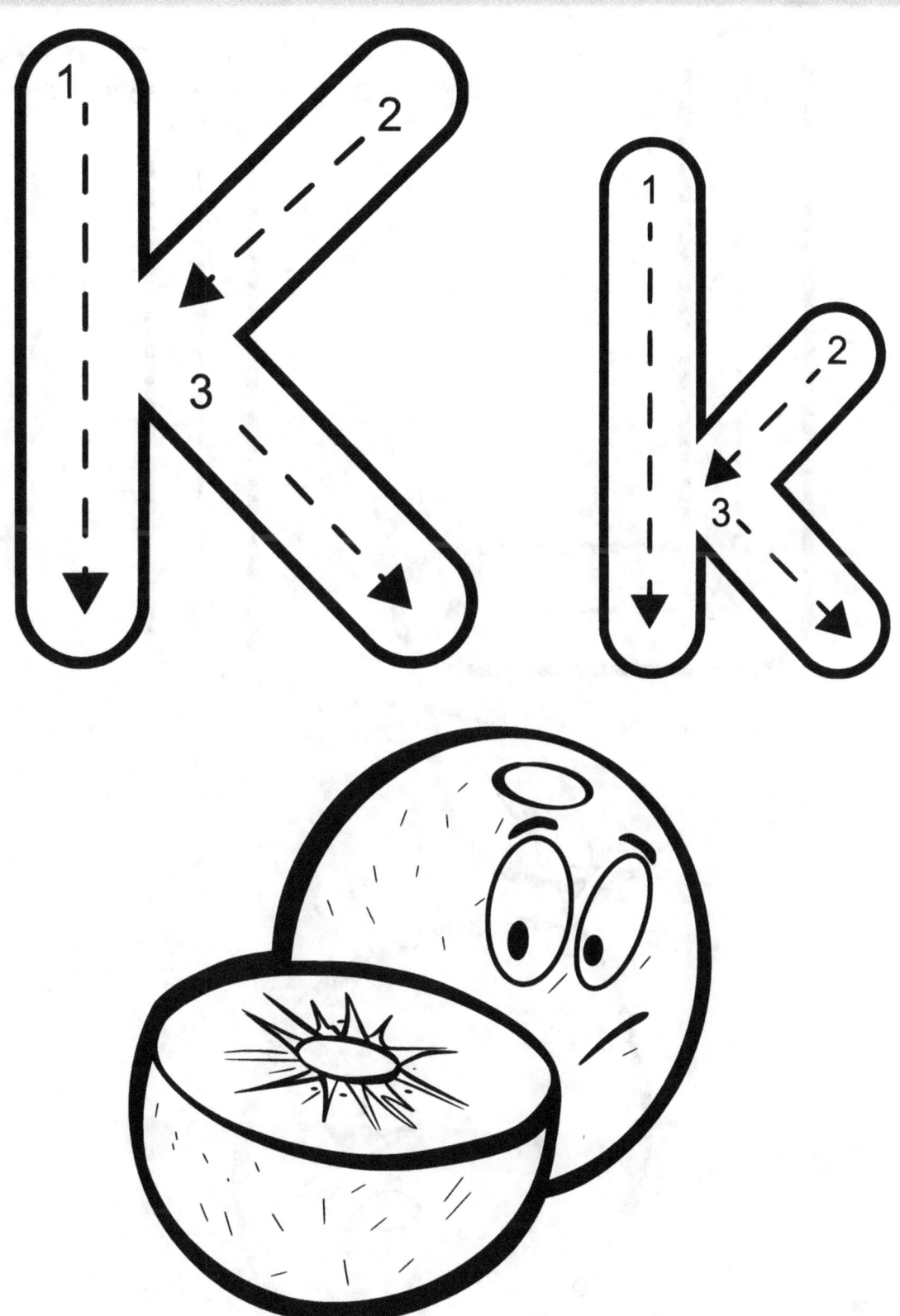

Answer: kiwi!

1

What fruit or vegetable
starts with this letter?

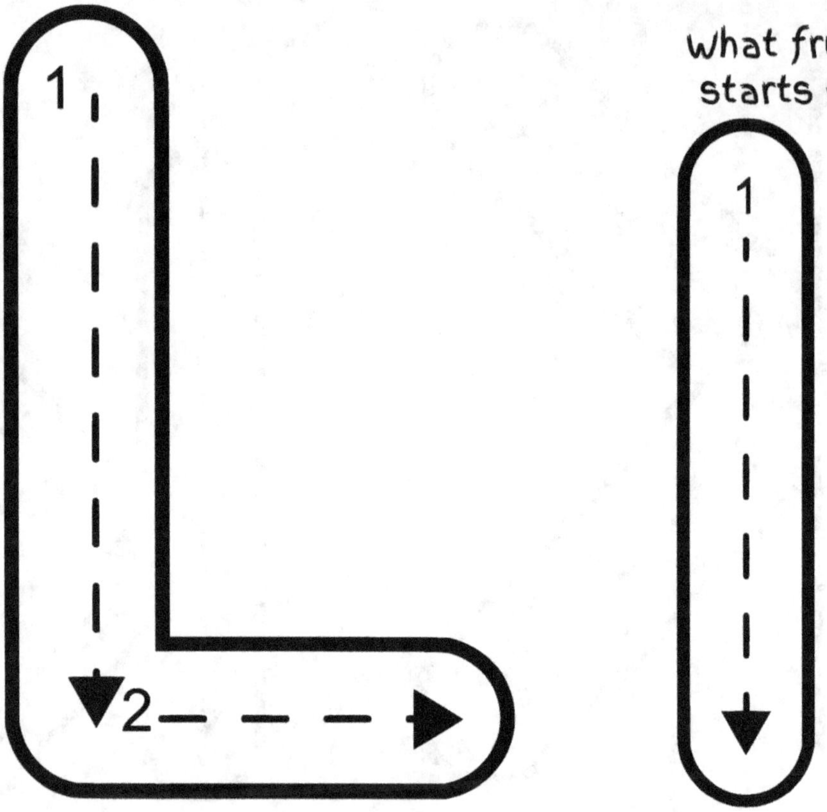

1

L

2

Answer: Lemon

BEEZUS BEE'S Letter Tracing Coloring Worksheets © 2024 Tuttle N Friends media LLC

BEEZUS BEE'S Letter Tracing Worksheets

© 2024 Tuttle N Friends media LLC

Answer: Mango

What fruit or vegetable starts with the letter..?

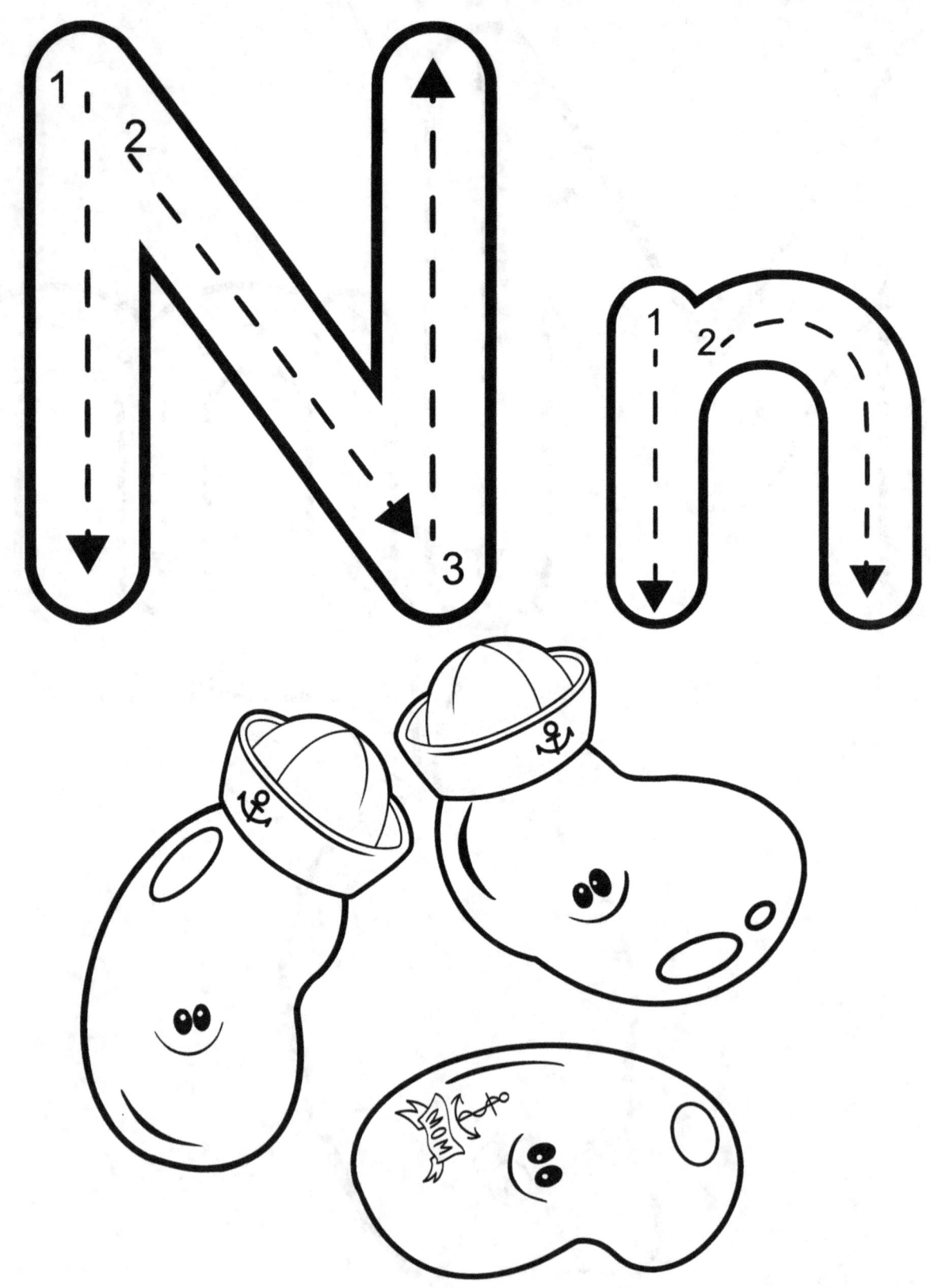

Answer: Navy Beans

BEEZUS BEE'S Letter Tracing Coloring Worksheets © 2024 Tuttle N Friends media LLC

Answer: orange

Answer: pear

BEEZUS BEE'S Letter Tracing Worksheets

© 2024 Tuttle N Friends media LLC

Answer: Queen Tahiti pineapple

Answer: Rutabaga

© 2024 Tuttle N Friends media LLC

Answer: Serrano pepper

© 2024 Tuttle N Friends media LLC

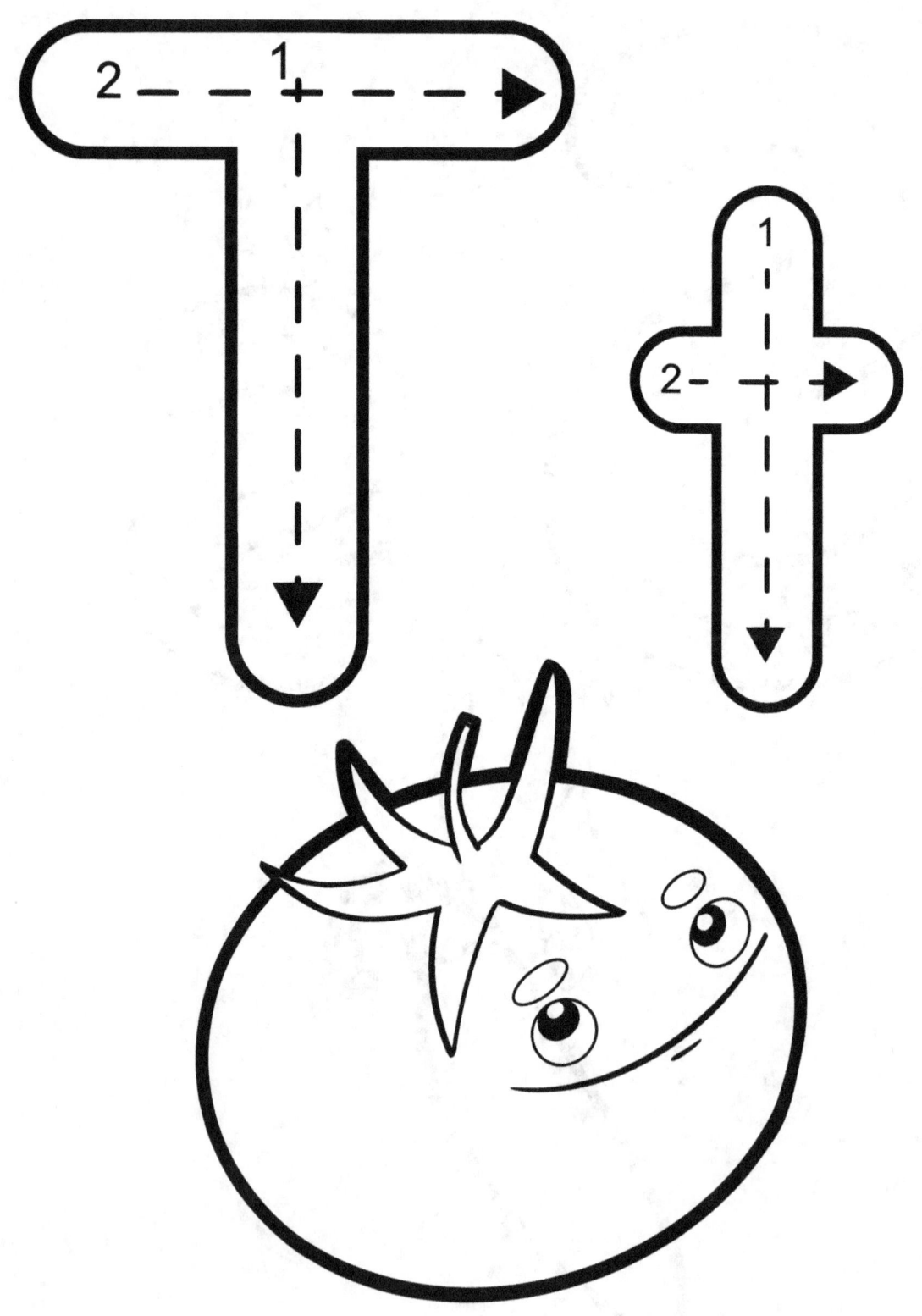

Answer: Tomato

tuttlenfriendsmedia.com

BEEZUS BEE'S Letter Tracing Coloring Worksheets

© 2024 Tuttle N Friends media LLC

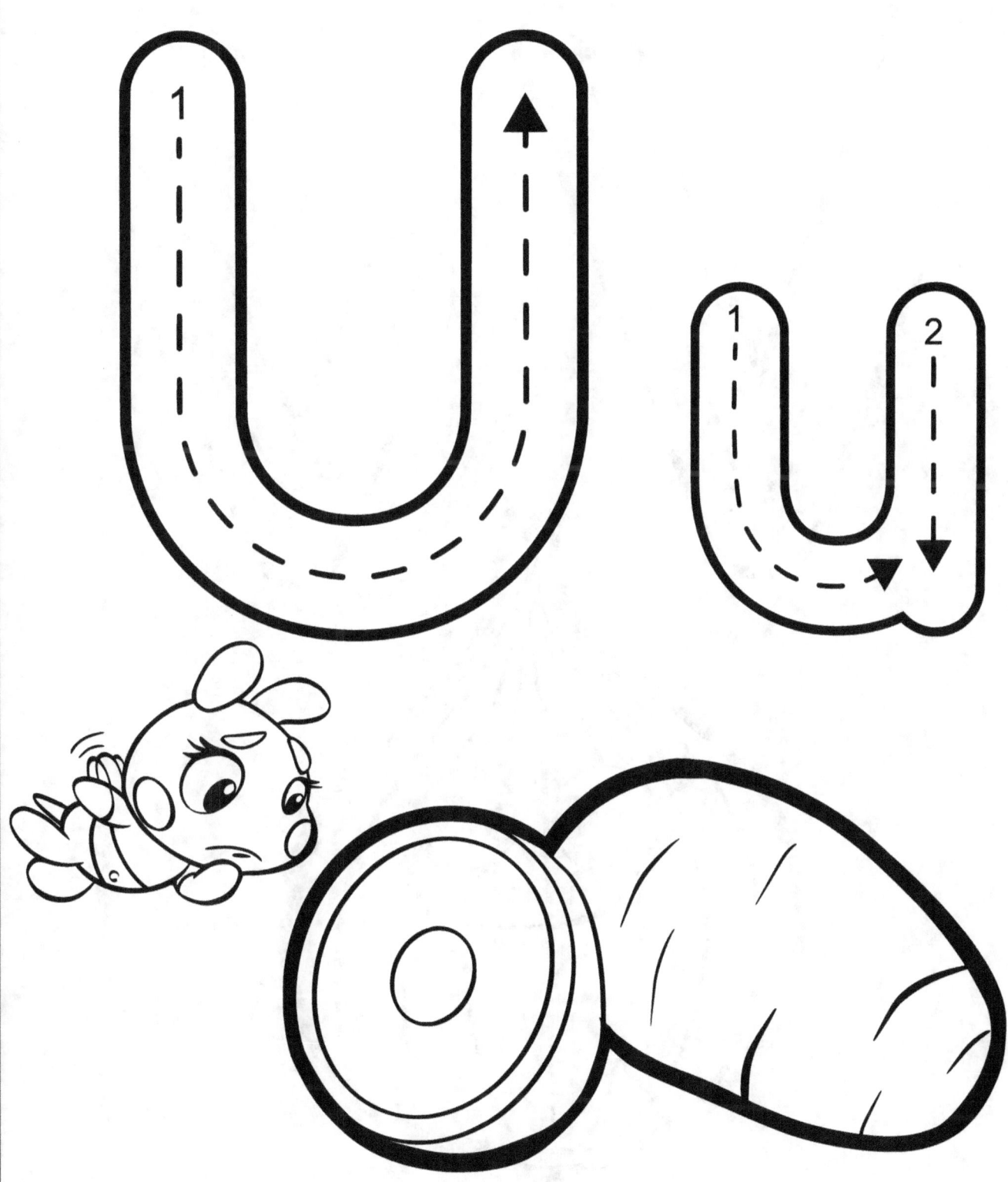

Answer: Ube

© 2024 Tuttle N Friends media LLC

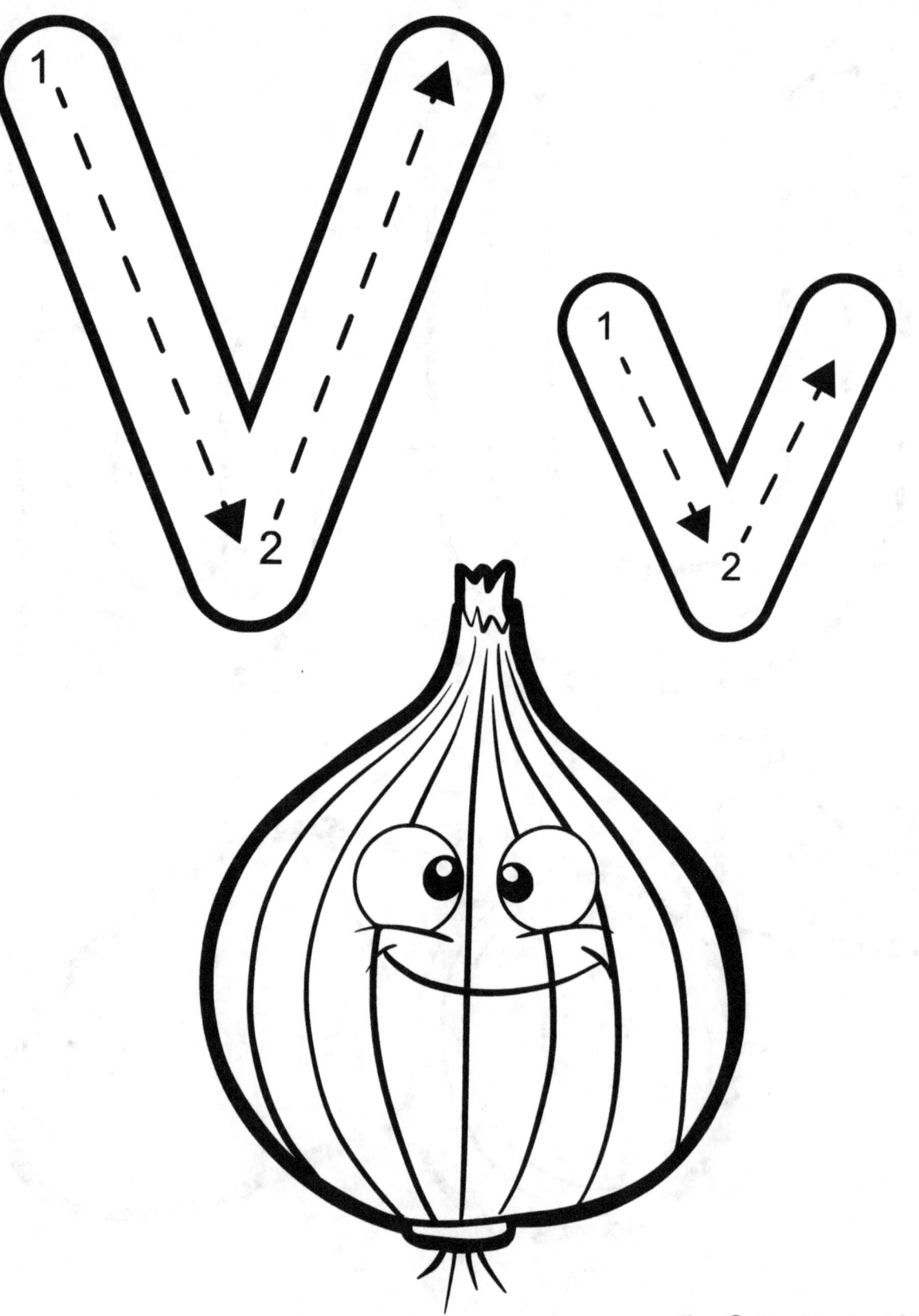

BEEZUS BEE'S Letter Tracing coloring Worksheets

© 2024 Tuttle N Friends media LLC

Answer: Vidalia Onion

What fruit or vegetable starts with the letter..?

Answer: Watermelon

tuttlenfriendsmedia.com   BEEZUS BEE'S Letter Tracing Coloring Worksheets   © 2024 Tuttle N Friends media LLC

Answer: Ximenia

© 2024 Tuttle N Friends media LLC

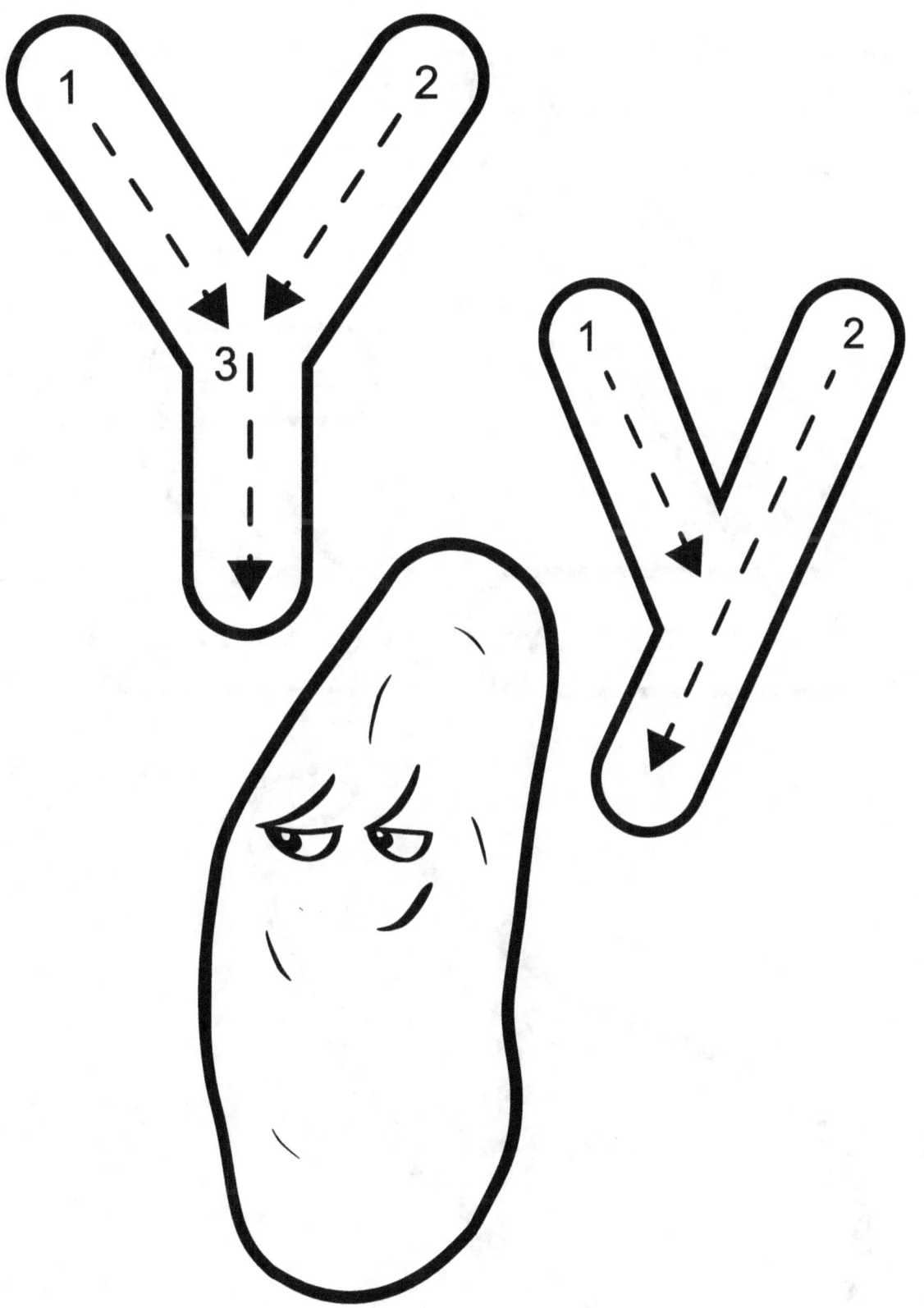

Answer: Yam

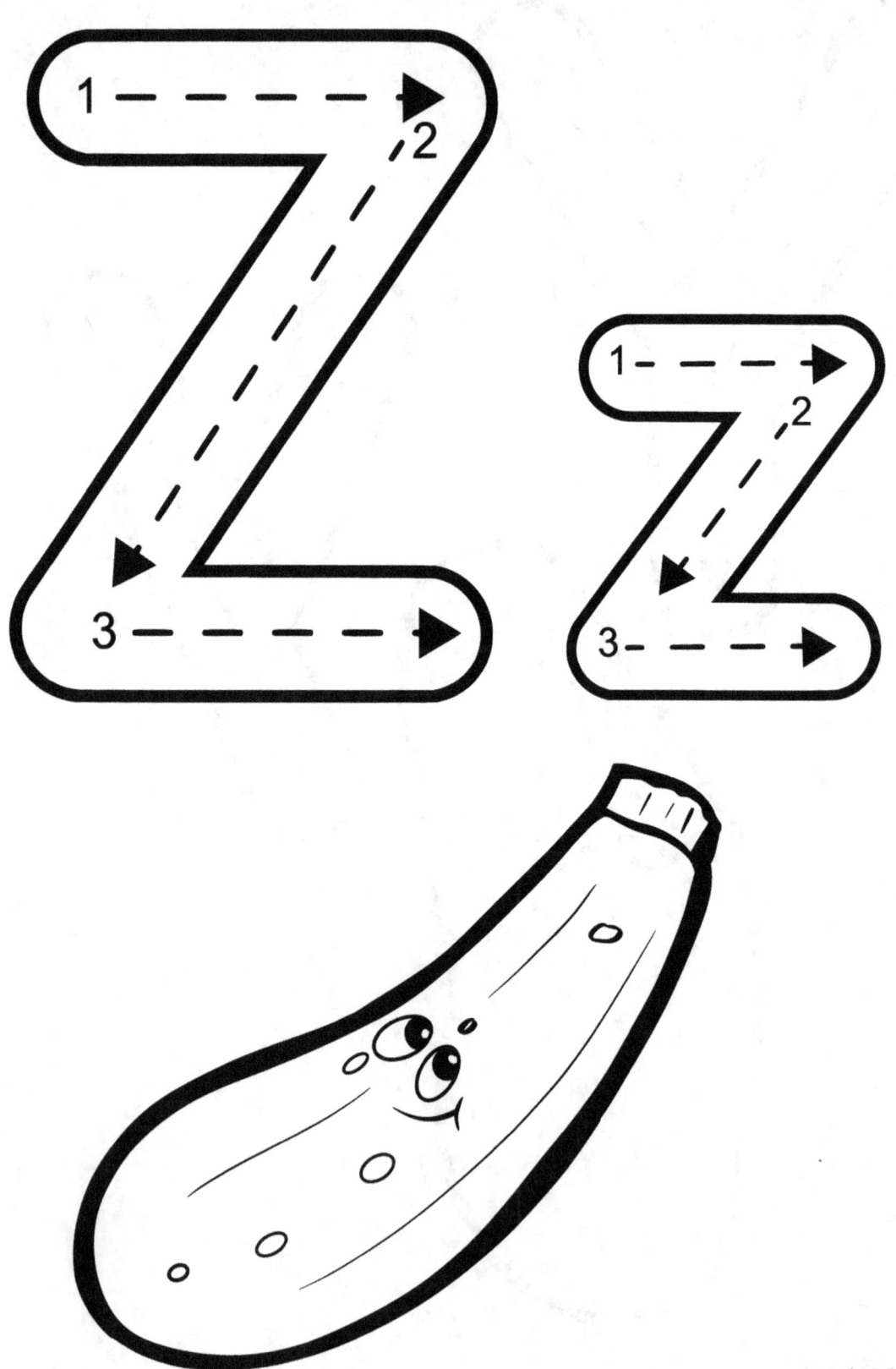

Answer: Zucchini!

A a

Name: _____

Alligator

Alien

A B C D E F G H I J K L M N O P Q R S T U V W X Y Z

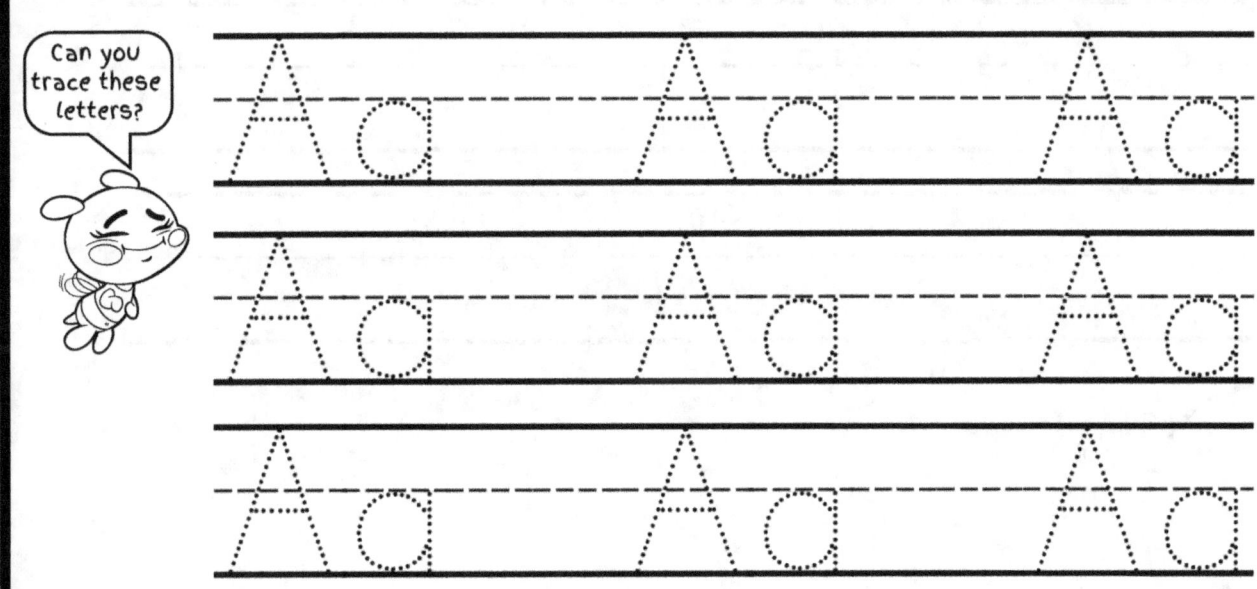

Can you trace these letters?

Aa Aa Aa

Aa Aa Aa

Aa Aa Aa

tuttlenfriendsmedia.com

BEEZUS BEE'S Letter Tracing Coloring Worksheets

© 2024 Tuttle N Friends media LLC

Aa   Aa   Aa

Aa   Aa   Aa

Aa   Aa   Aa

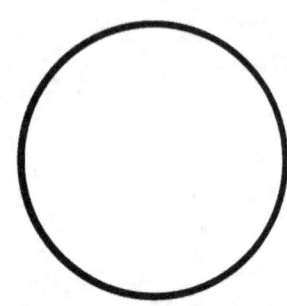

Can you write the letter below?

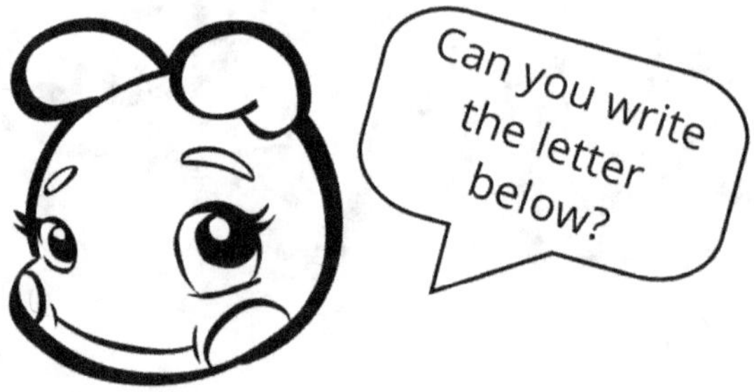

© 2024 Tuttle N Friends media LLC

Name: _____

Bunny

Balloons

A B C D E F G H I J K L M N O P Q R S T U V W X Y Z

Can you trace these letters?

Bb   Bb   Bb

Bb   Bb   Bb

Bb   Bb   Bb

tuttlenfriendsmedia.com

BEEZUS BEE'S Letter Tracing Coloring Worksheets

© 2024 Tuttle N Friends media LLC

Can you write the letter below?

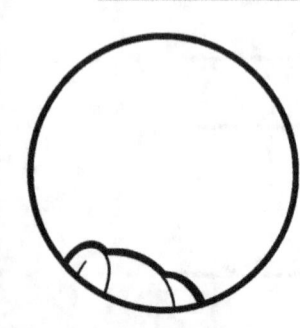

© 2024 Tuttle N Friends media LLC

C

Name: _____

Caterpillar

Cactus

A B **C** D E F G H I J K L M N O P Q R S T U V W X Y Z

Can you trace these letters?

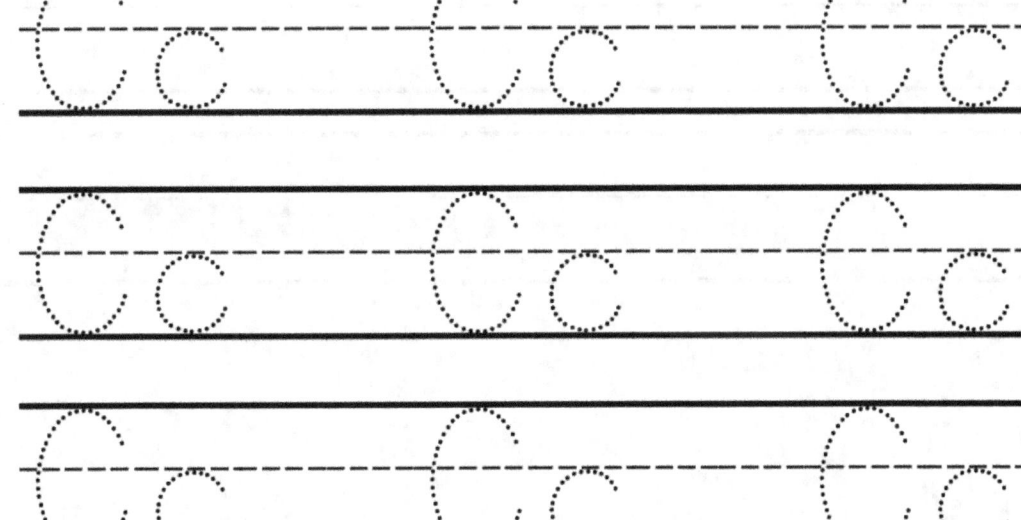

BEEZUS BEE'S Letter Tracing Coloring Worksheets

© 2024 Tuttle N Friends media LLC

BEEZUS BEE'S Letter Tracing ~~Work~~ Coloring sheets

Cc Cc Cc

Cc Cc Cc

Cc Cc Cc

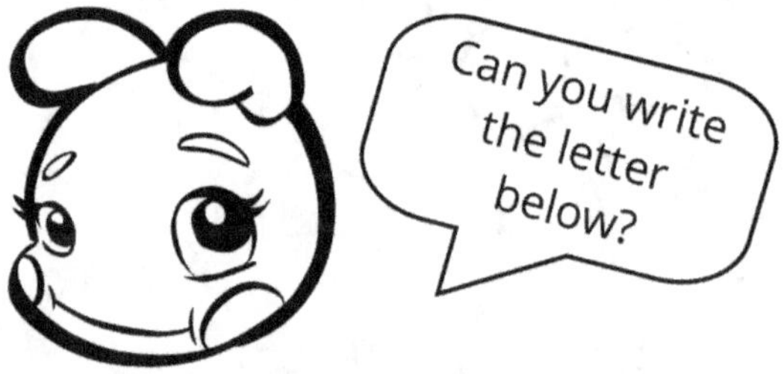
Can you write the letter below?

tuttlenfriendsmedia.com

© 2024 Tuttle N Friends media LLC

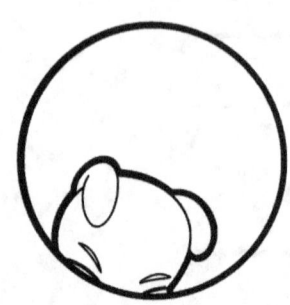

Name: _____

Ducky

Dinosaur

A B C **D** E F G H I J K L M N O P Q R S T U V W X Y Z

Can you trace these letters?

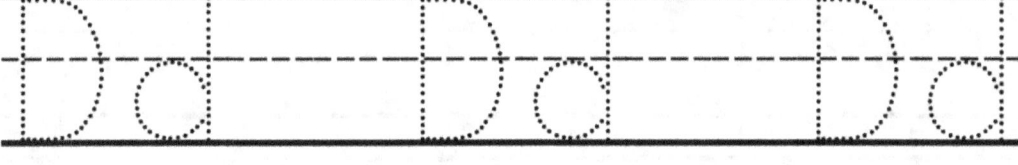

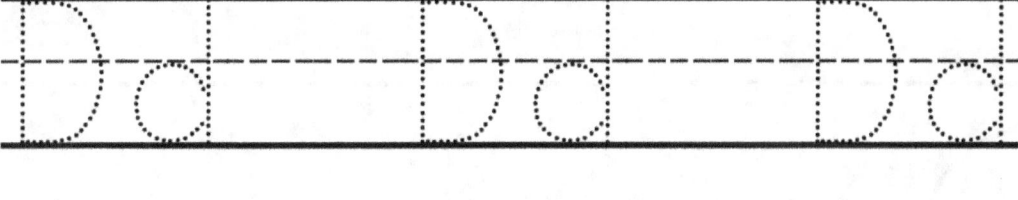

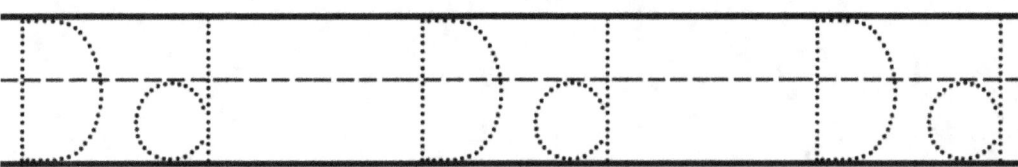

tuttlenfriendsmedia.com

BEEZUS BEE'S Letter Tracing Coloring Worksheets

© 2024 Tuttle N Friends media LLC

Dd   Dd   Dd

Dd   Dd   Dd

Dd   Dd   Dd

Can you write the letter below?

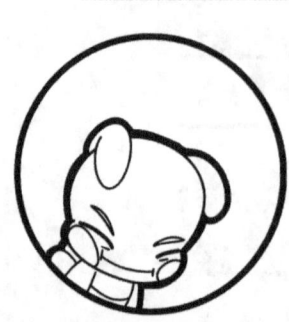

© 2024 Tuttle N Friends media LLC

E E e

Elephant

Earth

A B C D E F G H I J K L M N O P Q R S T U V W X Y Z

Can you trace these letters?

e   e   e

e   e   e

e   e   e

BEEZUS BEE'S Letter Tracing Coloring Worksheets © 2024 Tuttle N Friends media LLC

E e E e E e

E e E e E e

E e E e E e

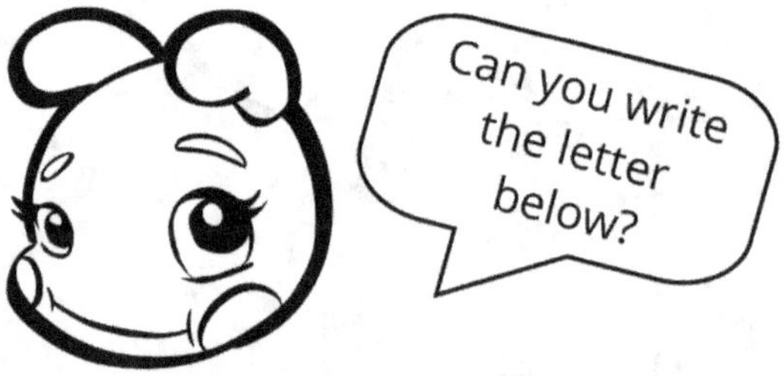
Can you write
the letter
below?

© 2024 Tuttle N Friends media LLC

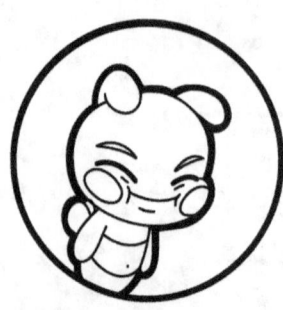

Name: _____

Fruit

Flowers

A B C D E **F** G H I J K L M N O P Q R S T U V W X Y Z

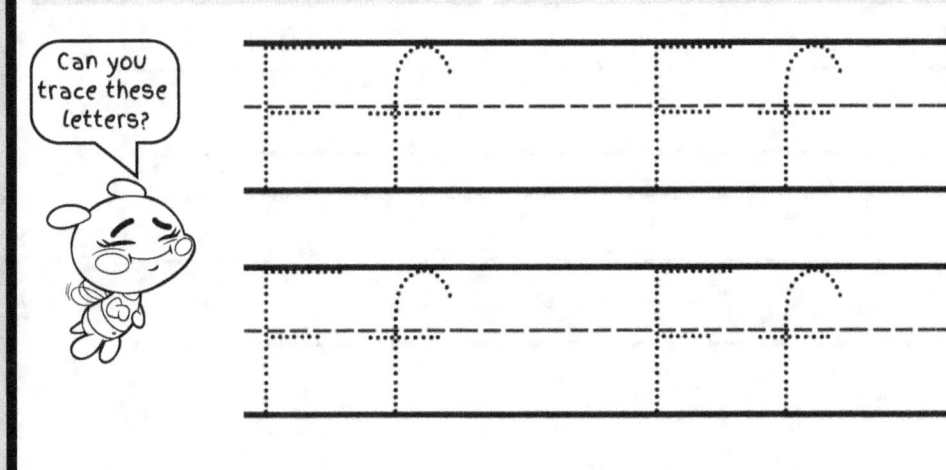

Can you trace these letters?

tuttlenfriendsmedia.com

BEEZUS BEE'S Letter Tracing Coloring Worksheets

© 2024 Tuttle N Friends media LLC

Ff Ff Ff

Ff Ff Ff

Ff Ff Ff

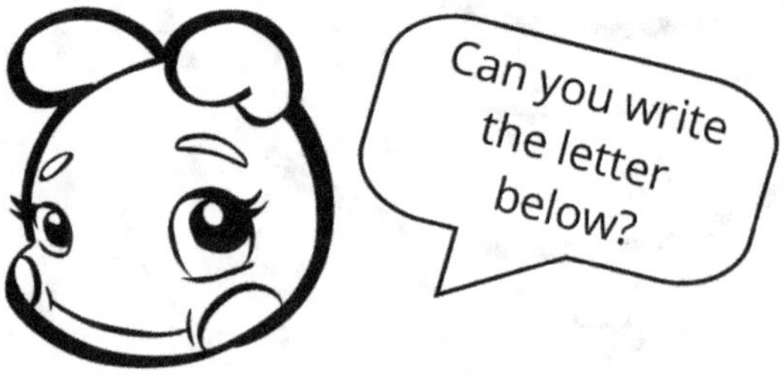
Can you write the letter below?

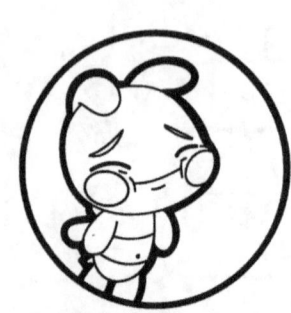

© 2024 Tuttle N Friends media LLC

Name: _____

Gingerbread People

Goldfish

A B C D E F **G** H I J K L M N O P Q R S T U V W X Y Z

Can you trace these letters?

Gg Gg Gg

Gg Gg Gg

Gg Gg Gg

tuttlenfriendsmedia.com

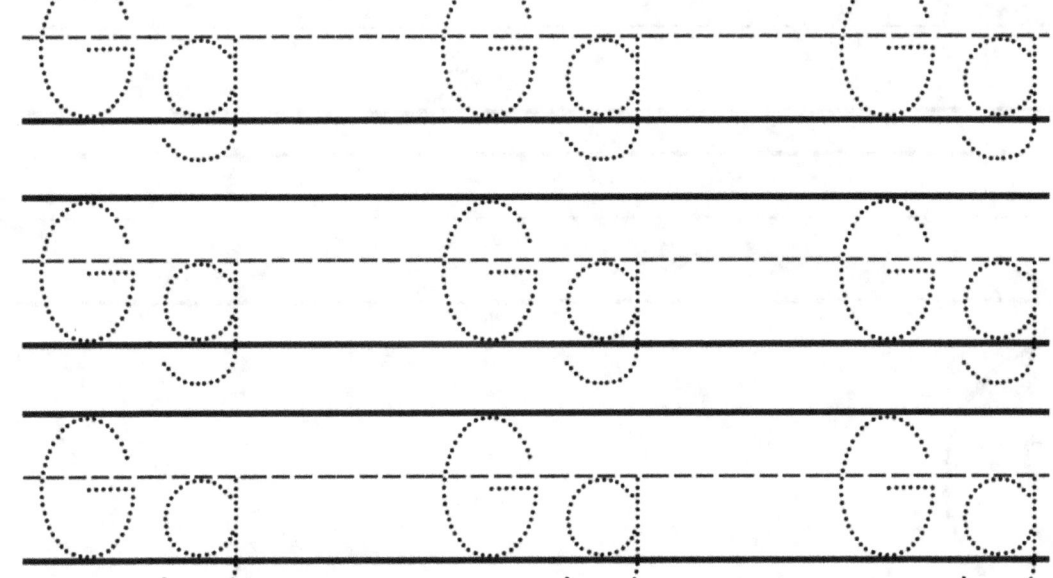

BEEZUS BEE'S Letter Tracing Coloring Worksheets

© 2024 Tuttle N Friends media LLC

Gg Gg Gg

Gg Gg Gg

Gg Gg Gg

Can you write the letter below?

© 2024 Tuttle N Friends media LLC

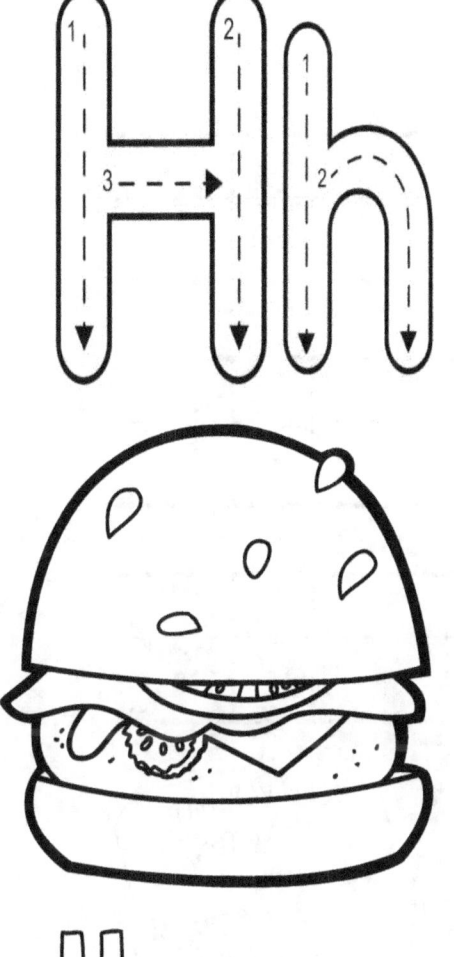

Name: _____

Hamburger

House

A B C D E F G **H** I J K L M N O P Q R S T U V W X Y Z

tuttlenfriendsmedia.com

Can you trace these letters?

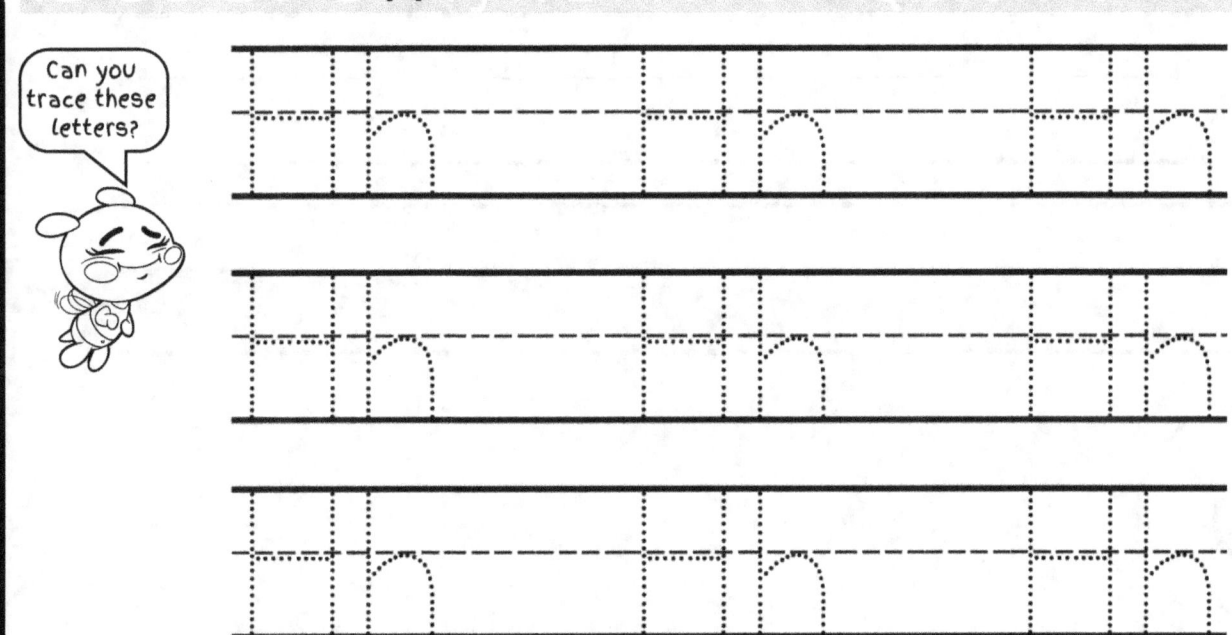

BEEZUS BEE'S Letter Tracing Coloring Worksheets

© 2024 Tuttle N Friends media LLC

BEEZUS BEE'S Letter Tracing ~~Work~~coloring sheets

Hh Hh Hh

Hh Hh Hh

Hh Hh Hh

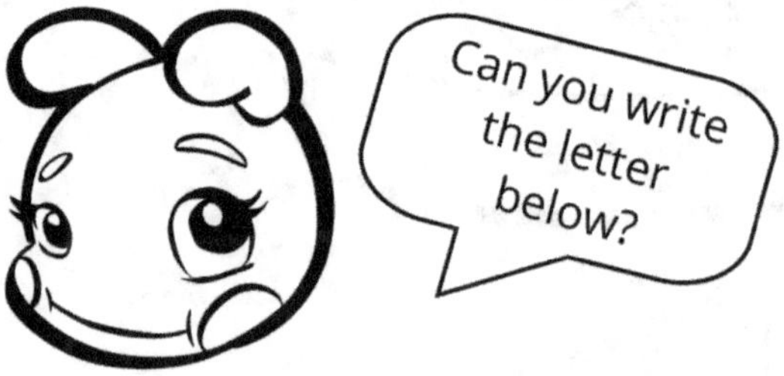
Can you write the letter below?

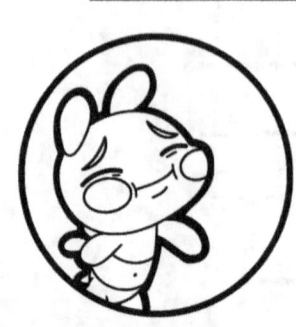

© 2024 Tuttle N Friends media LLC

Name: _____

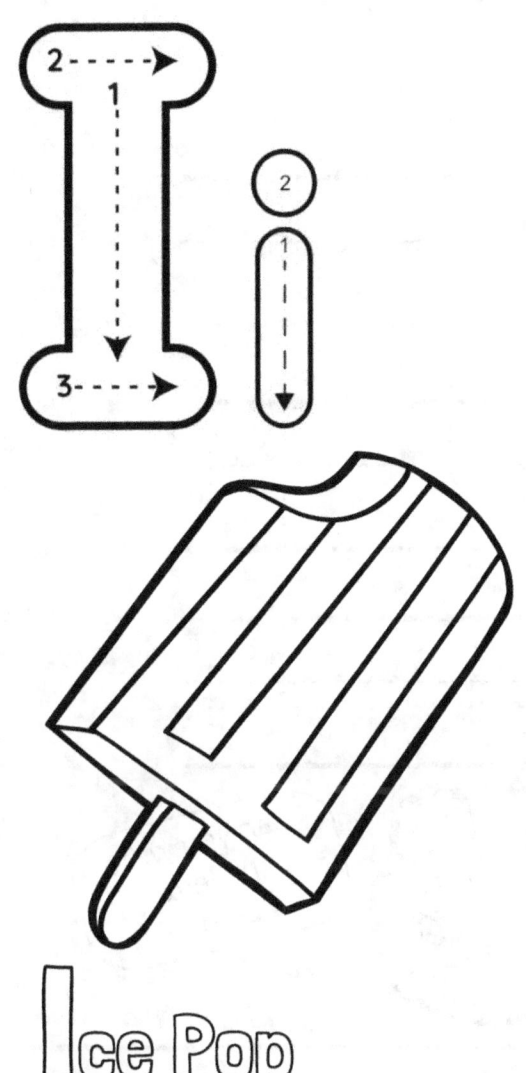

Ice Pop

Ice Cream

A B C D E F G H I J K L M N O P Q R S T U V W X Y Z

Can you trace these letters?

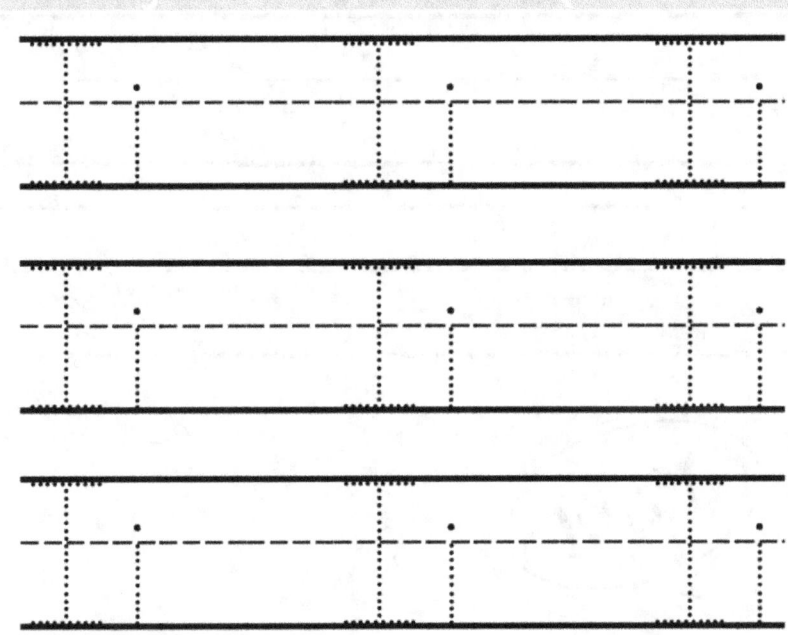

BEEZUS BEE'S Letter Tracing Coloring Worksheets © 2024 Tuttle N Friends media LLC

Can you write the letter below?

Yay!

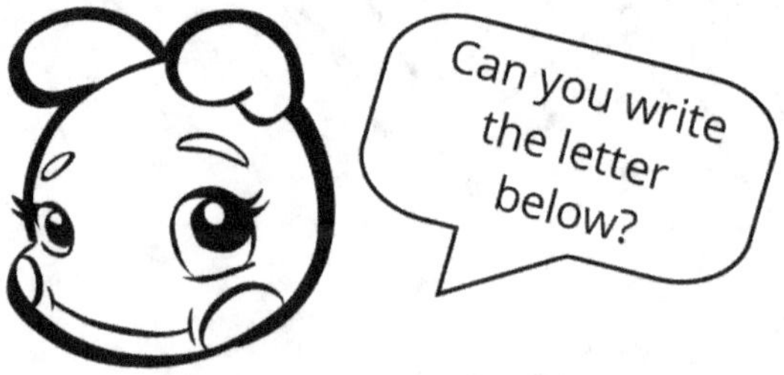

© 2024 Tuttle N Friends media LLC

Name: _____

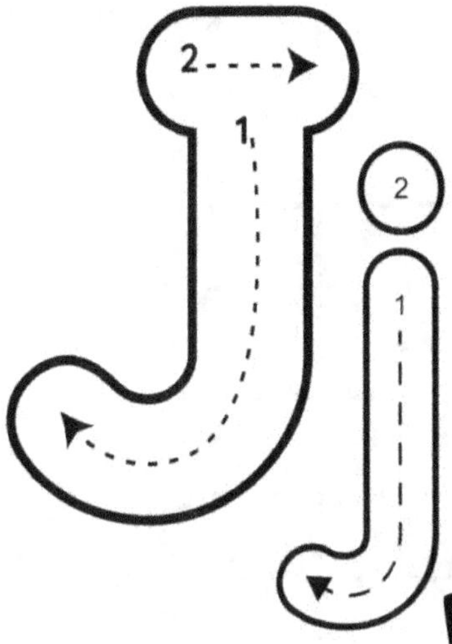

J j

2 ---->
1
2
1

Juice

Juice Box

Jump rope

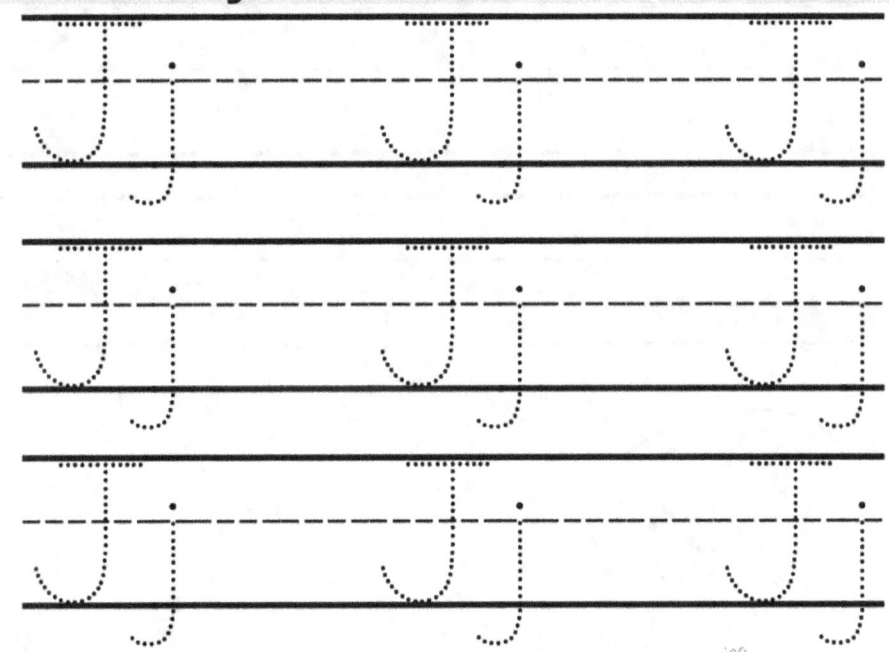

A B C D E F G H I **J** K L M N O P Q R S T U V W X Y Z

Can you trace these letters?

BEEZUS BEE'S Letter Tracing Coloring Worksheets

© 2024 Tuttle N Friends media LLC

Jj Jj Jj

Jj Jj Jj

Jj Jj Jj

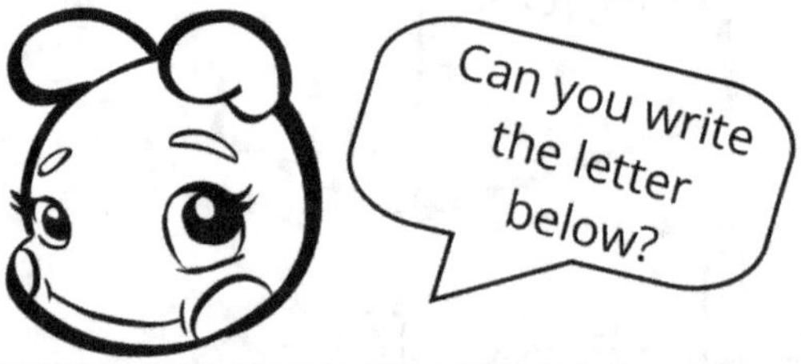

Can you write the letter below?

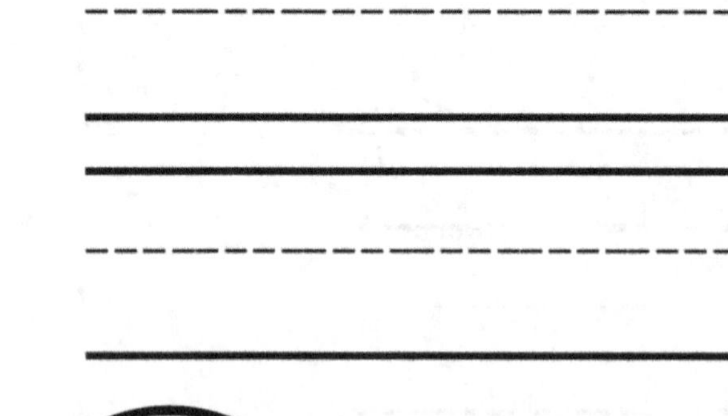

© 2024 Tuttle N Friends media LLC

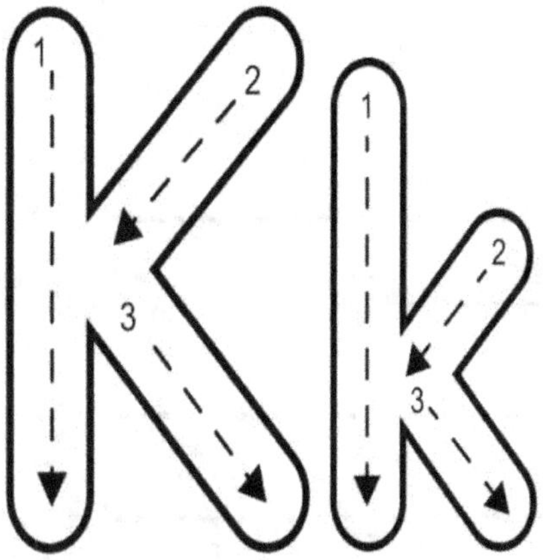

K k

Name: _____

Koala

Kangaroo

A B C D E F G H I J **K** L M N O P Q R S T U V W X Y Z

Can you trace these letters?

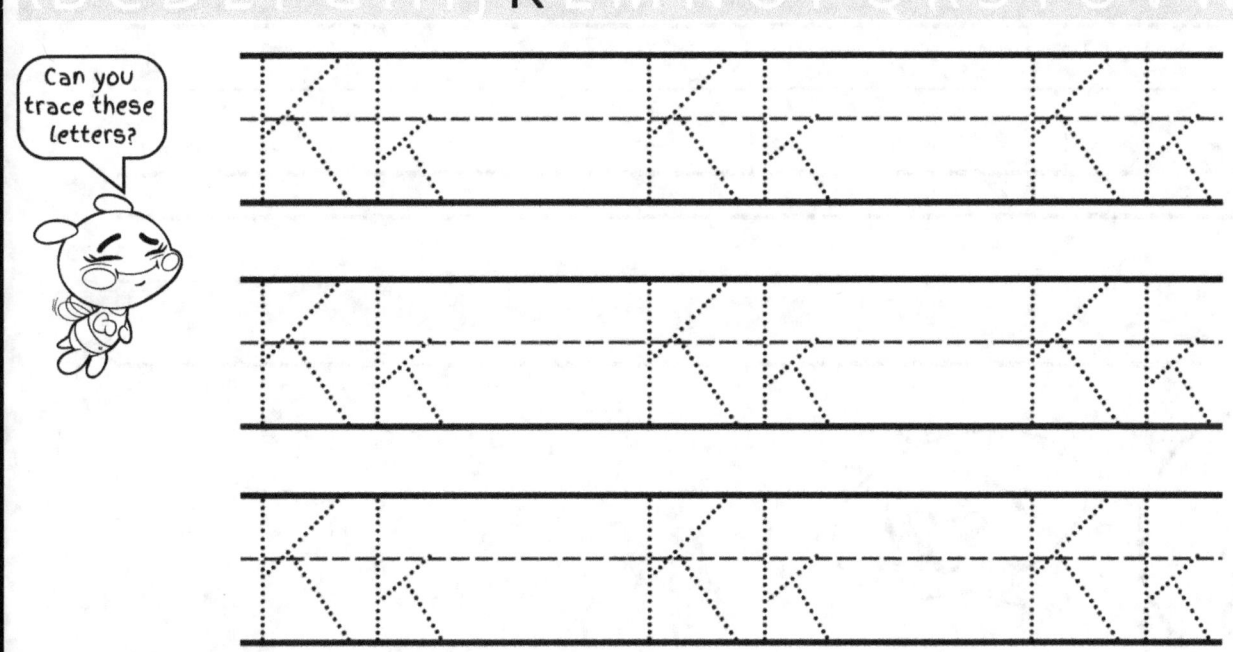

tuttlenfriendsmedia.com   BEEZUS BEE'S Letter Tracing Coloring Worksheets   © 2024 Tuttle N Friends media LLC

Kk — Kk — Kk

Kk — Kk — Kk

Kk — Kk — Kk

Can you write the letter below?

Yay!

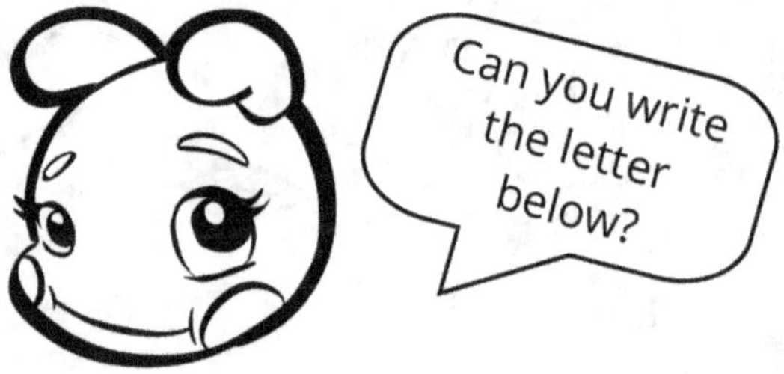

© 2024 Tuttle N Friends media LLC

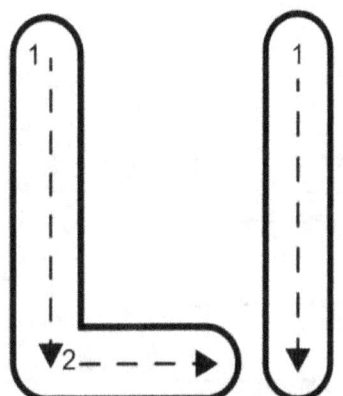

Name: _____

Lady Bugs

Lion

A B C D E F G H I J K **L** M N O P Q R S T U V W X Y Z

Can you trace these letters?

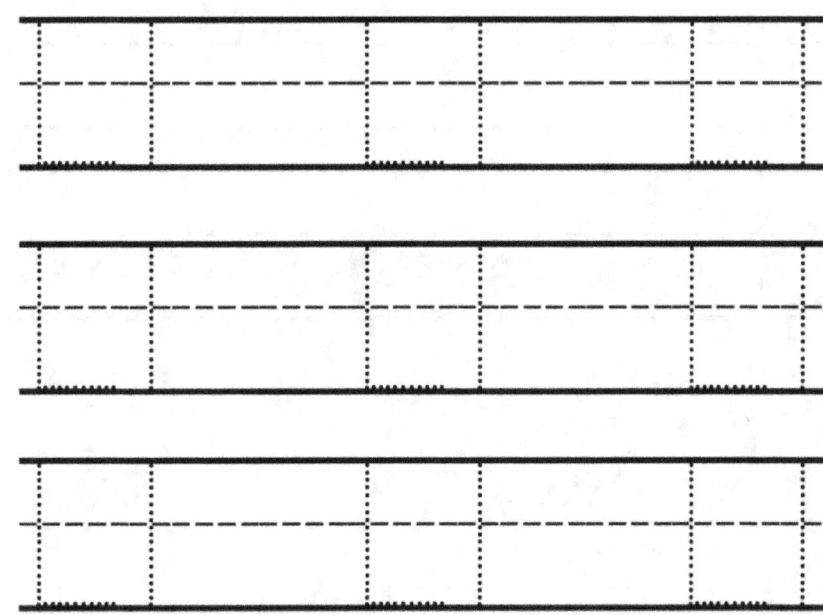

tuttlenfriendsmedia.com

BEEZUS BEE'S Letter Tracing Worksheets

© 2024 Tuttle N Friends media LLC

Can you write the letter below?

Yay!

© 2024 Tuttle N Friends media LLC

Mm

Mermaid

Monster

A B C D E F G H I J K L **M** N O P Q R S T U V W X Y Z

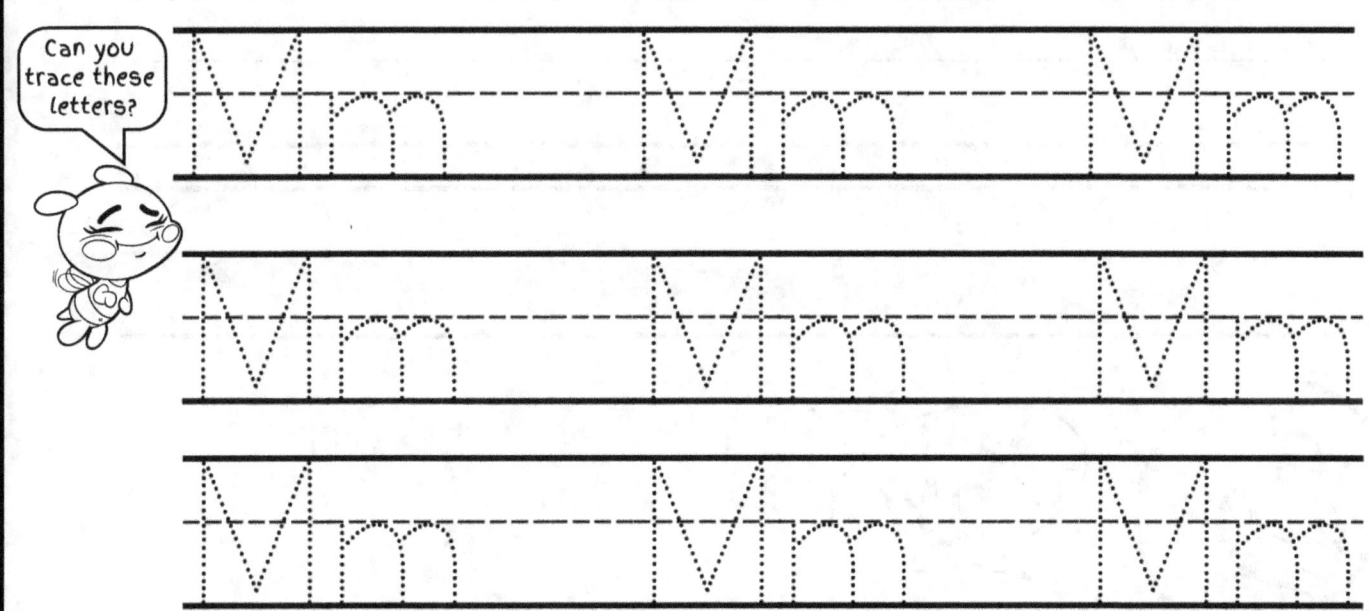

Can you trace these letters?

Mm   Mm   Mm

Mm   Mm   Mm

Mm   Mm   Mm

> Can you write the letter below?

Yay!

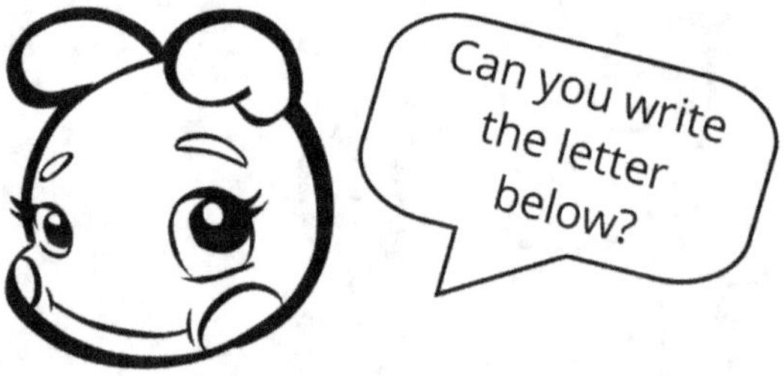

© 2024 Tuttle N Friends media LLC

N n

Name: _____

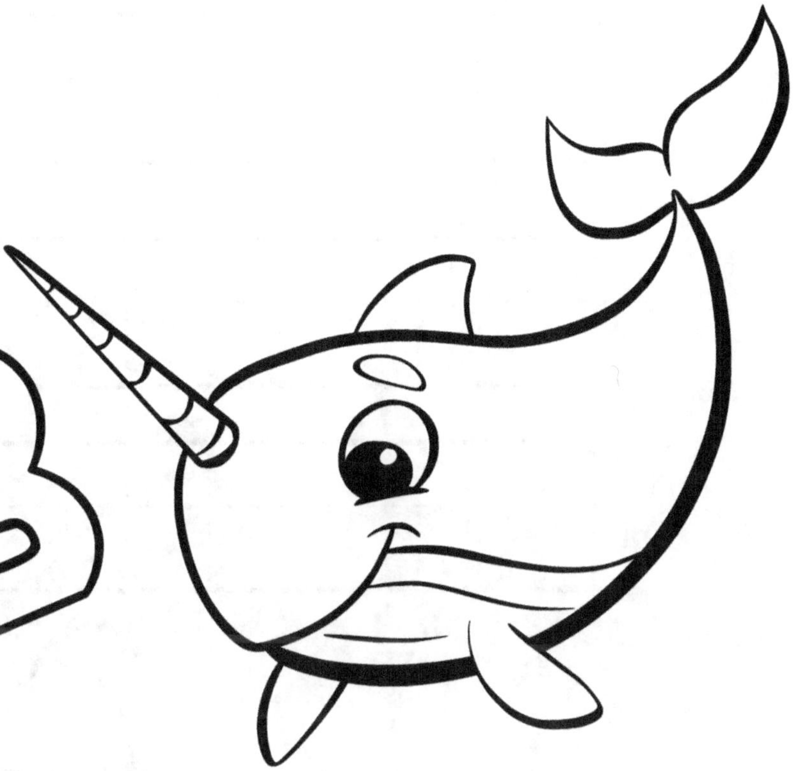

123
Numbers

Narwhal

N

Can you trace these letters?

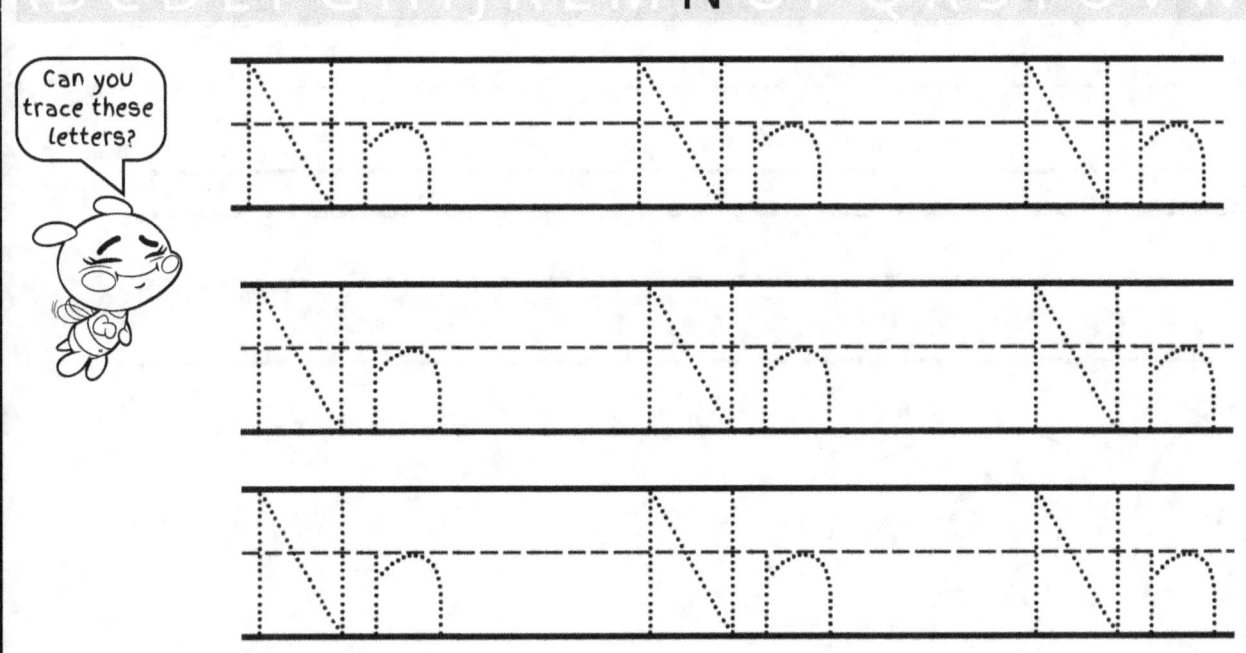

BEEZUS BEE'S Letter Tracing Coloring Worksheets

© 2024 Tuttle N Friends media LLC

Nn Nn Nn

Nn Nn Nn

Nn Nn Nn

Can you write the letter below?

Yay!

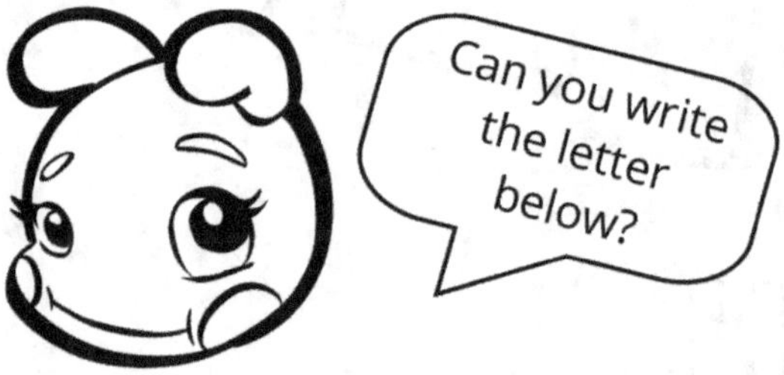

© 2024 Tuttle N Friends media LLC

Name: _____

Owl

Octopus

A B C D E F G H I J K L M N O P Q R S T U V W X Y Z

tuttlenfriendsmedia.com

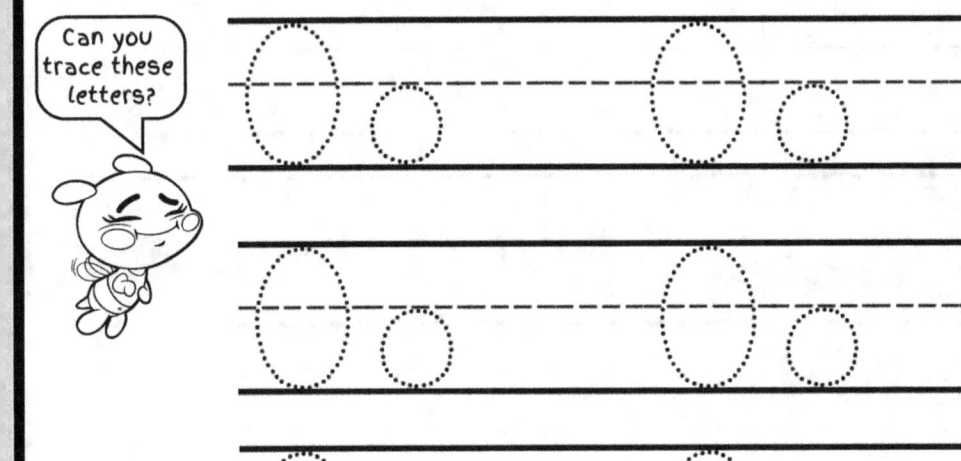

Can you trace these letters?

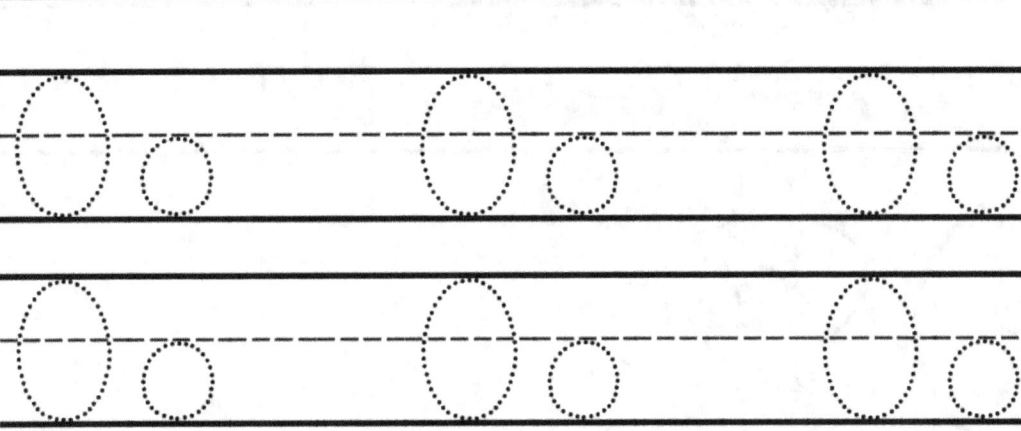

BEEZUS BEE'S Letter Tracing Coloring Worksheets

© 2024 Tuttle N Friends media LLC

Can you write the letter below?

Yay!

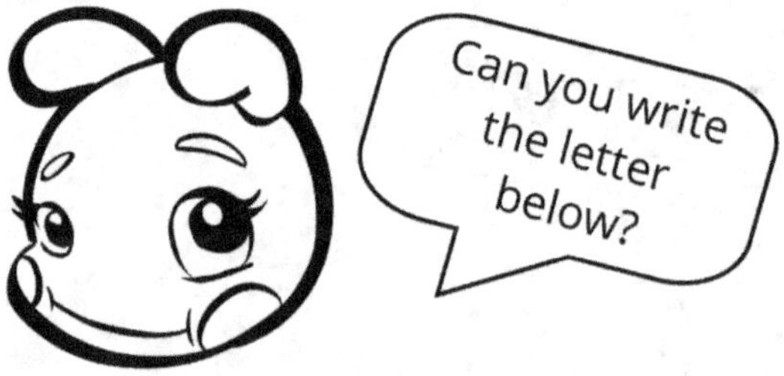

© 2024 Tuttle N Friends media LLC

Name: _____

© 2024 Tuttle N Friends media LLC

P p

Pig

Pizza

A B C D E F G H I J K L M N O P Q R S T U V W X Y Z

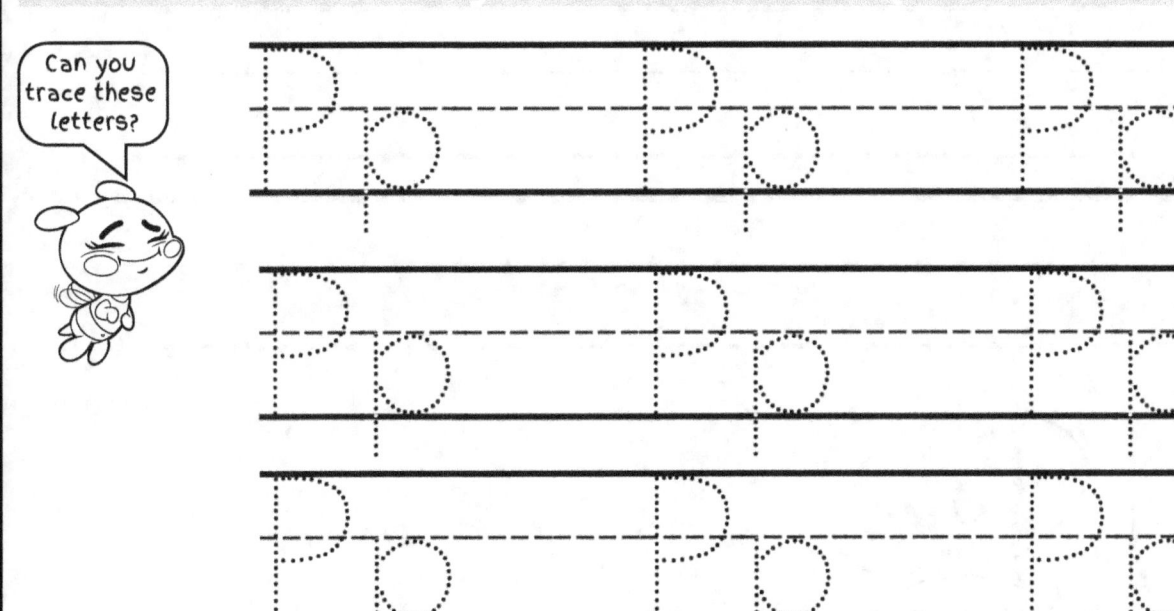

Can you trace these letters?

BEEZUS BEE'S Letter Tracing Coloring Worksheets

© 2024 Tuttle N Friends media LLC

Can you write the letter below?

Yay!

© 2024 Tuttle N Friends media LLC

Name: _____

Q q

Quail

Quiet Time

A B C D E F G H I J K L M N O P Q R S T U V W X Y Z

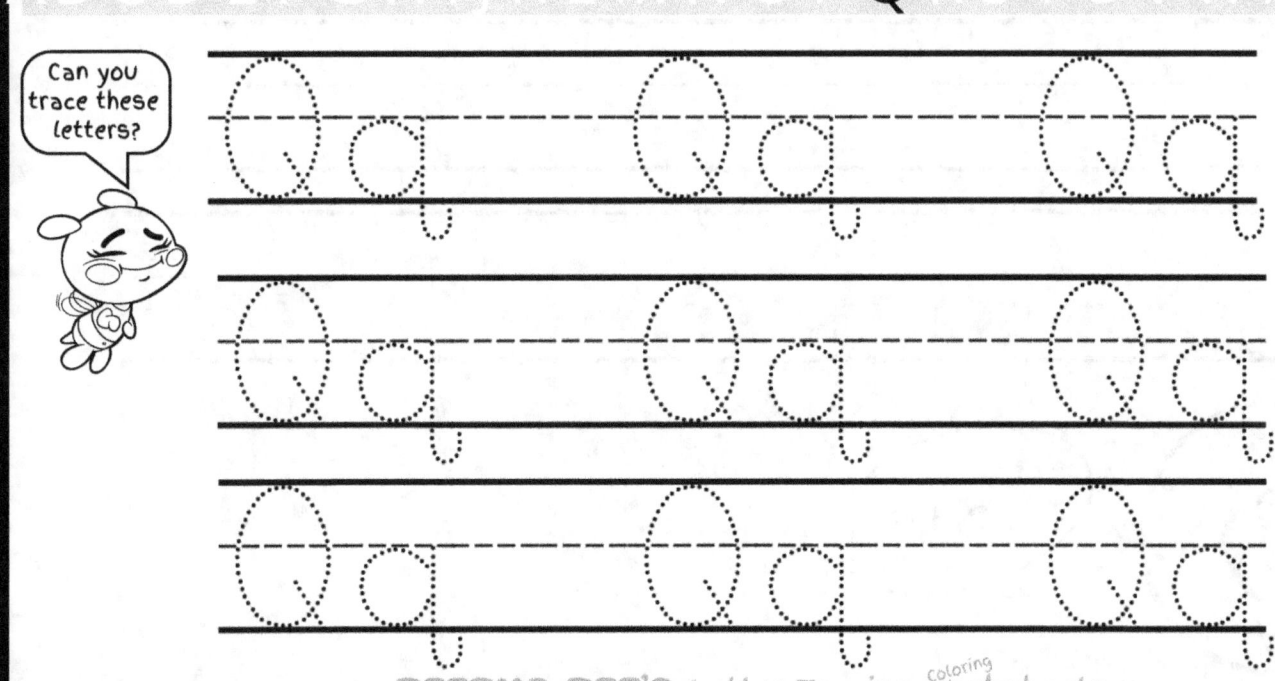

Can you trace these letters?

tuttlenfriendsmedia.com   BEEZUS BEE'S Letter Tracing Coloring Worksheets   © 2024 Tuttle N Friends media LLC

Qq Qq Qq

Qq Qq Qq

Qq Qq Qq

Can you write the letter below?

Yay!

© 2024 Tuttle N Friends media LLC

Name: _____

R Robot

R Rocket

A B C D E F G H I J K L M N O P Q R S T U V W X Y Z

Can you trace these letters?

Rr Rr Rr

Rr Rr Rr

Rr Rr Rr

BEEZUS BEE'S Letter Tracing Coloring Worksheets

© 2024 Tuttle N Friends media LLC

Rr   Rr   Rr

Rr   Rr   Rr

Rr   Rr   Rr

Can you write the letter below?

Yay!

© 2024 Tuttle N Friends media LLC

© 2024 Tuttle N Friends media LLC

S s

Seal

Sneaker

A B C D E F G H I J K L M N O P Q R **S** T U V W X Y Z

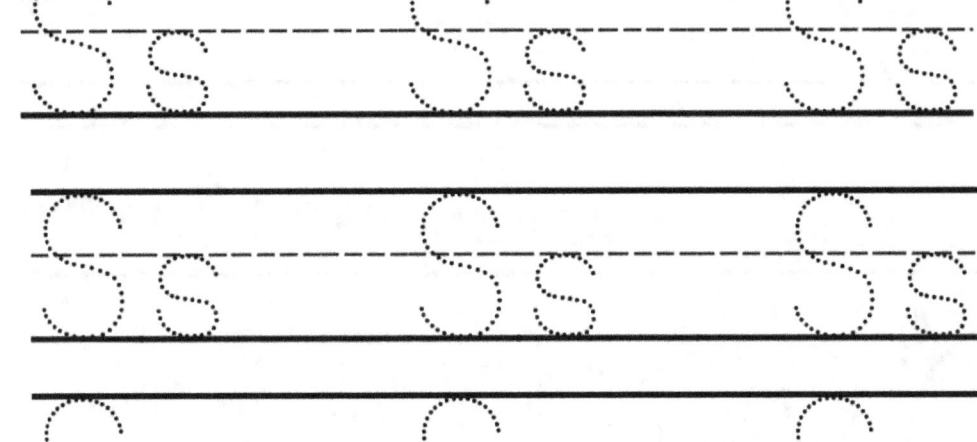

Can you trace these letters?

S s   S s   S s

S s   S s   S s

S s   S s   S s

Ss Ss Ss

Ss Ss Ss

Ss Ss Ss

Can you write the letter below?

Yay!

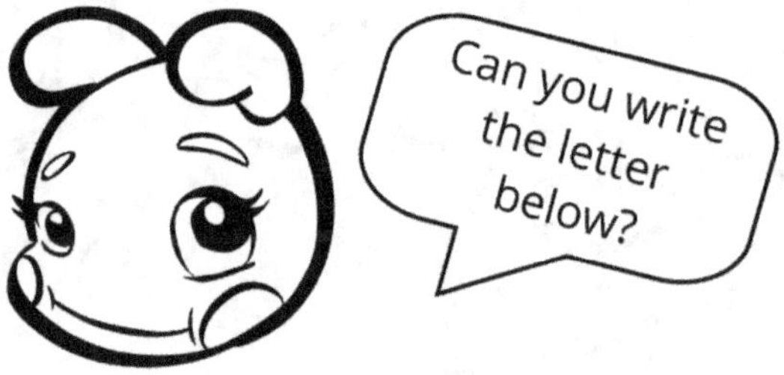

© 2024 Tuttle N Friends media LLC

Name: _____

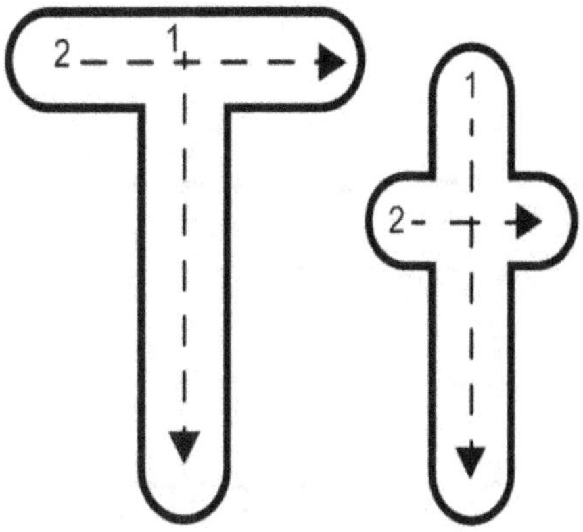

T T t

Teddy Bear

Tree

A B C D E F G H I J K L M N O P Q R S T U V W X Y Z

Can you trace these letters?

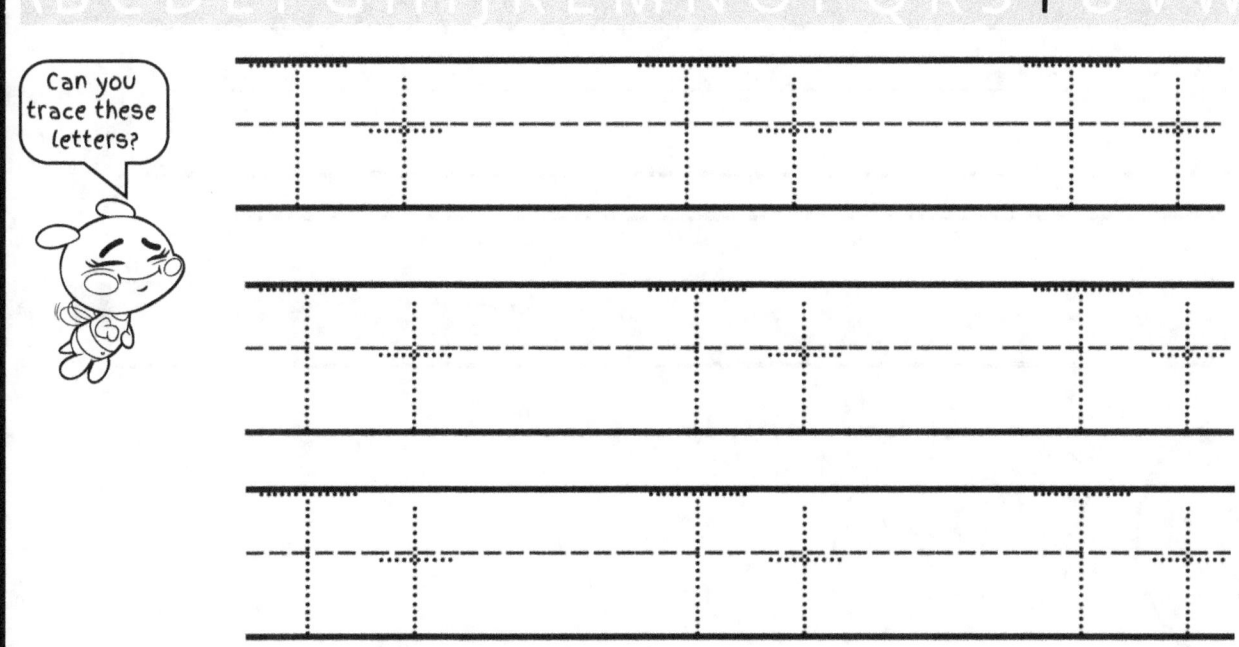

BEEZUS BEE'S Letter Tracing coloring Worksheets

© 2024 Tuttle N Friends media LLC

Can you write the letter below?

Yay!

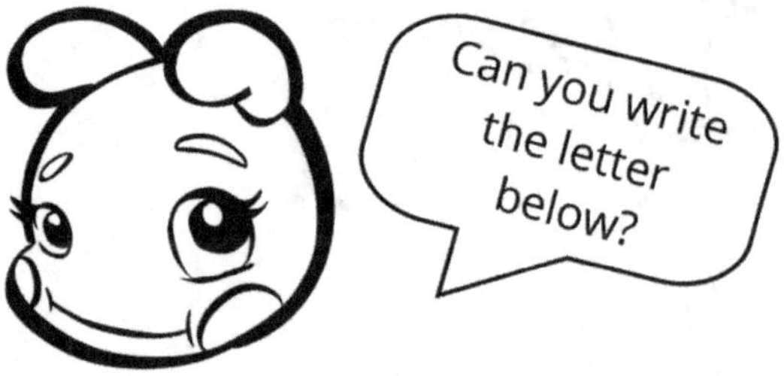

© 2024 Tuttle N Friends media LLC

U u

Name: _____

U

Umbrella

Unicorn

A B C D E F G H I J K L M N O P Q R S T **U** V W X Y Z

Can you trace these letters?

BEEZUS BEE'S Letter Tracing ~~coloring~~ Worksheets

© 2024 Tuttle N Friends media LLC

Uu Uu Uu

Uu Uu Uu

Uu Uu Uu

Can you write the letter below?

Yay!

© 2024 Tuttle N Friends media LLC

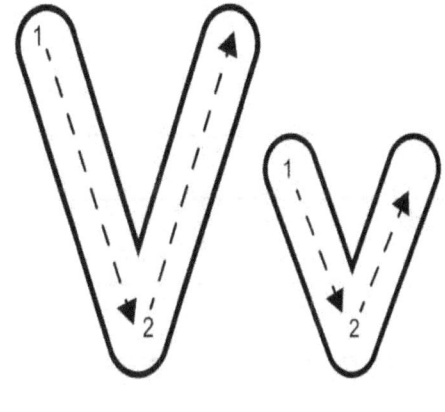

Name: _____

Vegetables

Violin

A B C D E F G H I J K L M N O P Q R S T U **V** W X Y Z

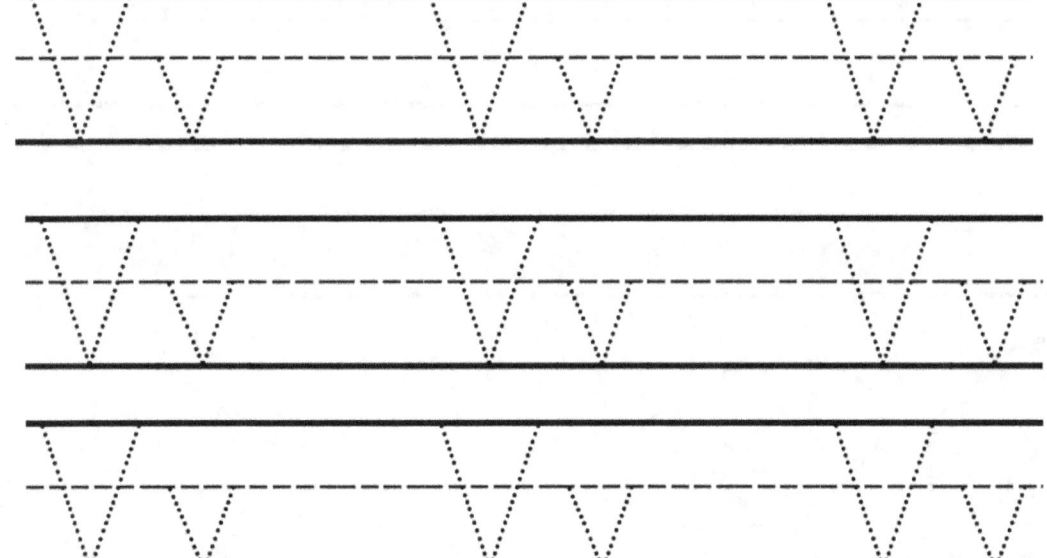

Can you trace these letters?

BEEZUS BEE'S Letter Tracing Coloring Worksheets

© 2024 Tuttle N Friends media LLC

Can you write the letter below?

Yay!

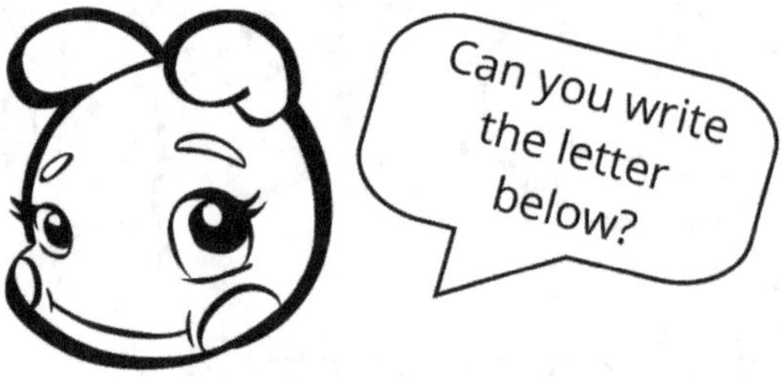

© 2024 Tuttle N Friends media LLC

Name: _____

Whistle

Worm

A B C D E F G H I J K L M N O P Q R S T U V **W** X Y Z

Can you trace these letters?

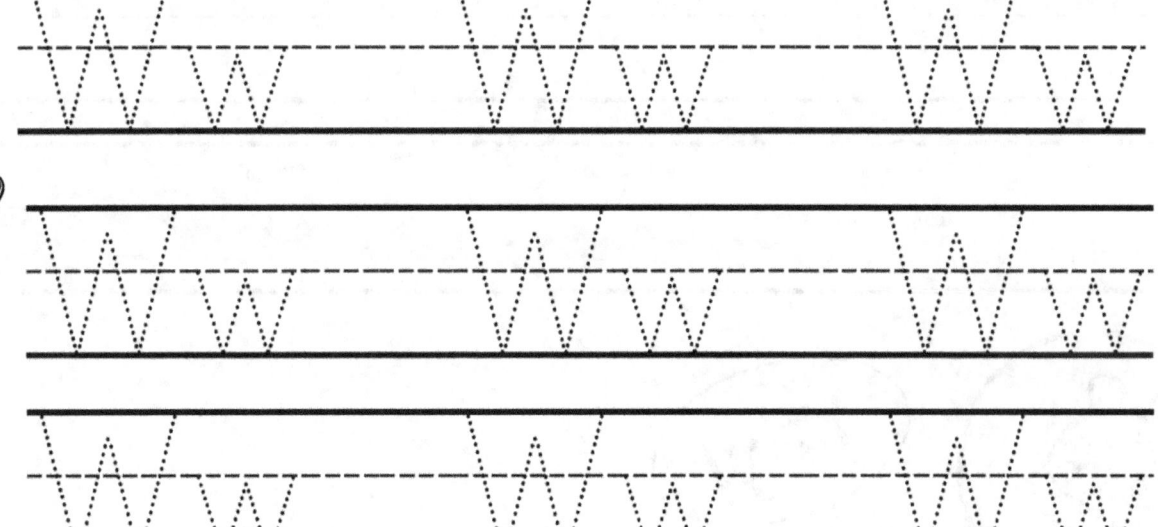

BEEZUS BEE'S Letter Tracing Coloring Worksheets

© 2024 Tuttle N Friends media LLC

Can you write the letter below?

Yay!

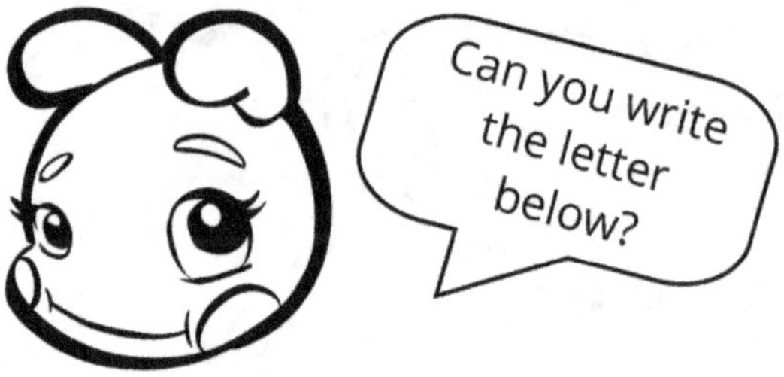

© 2024 Tuttle N Friends media LLC

Name: _____

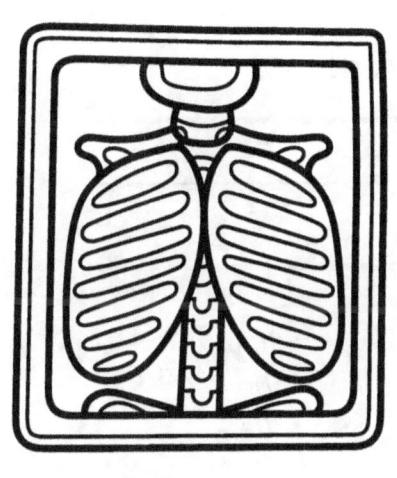

X-ray

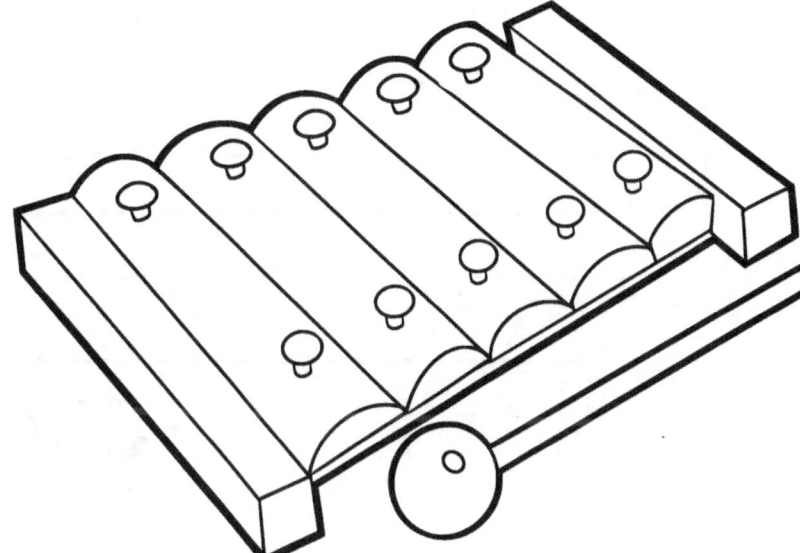

Xylophone

A B C D E F G H I J K L M N O P Q R S T U V W X Y Z

Can you trace these letters?

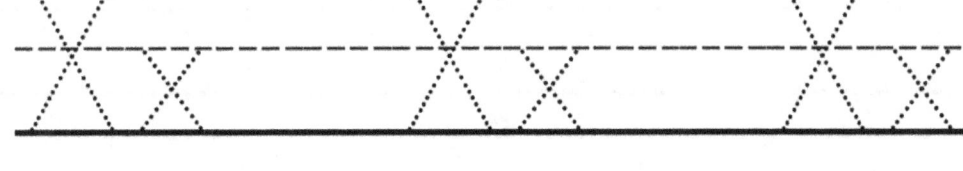

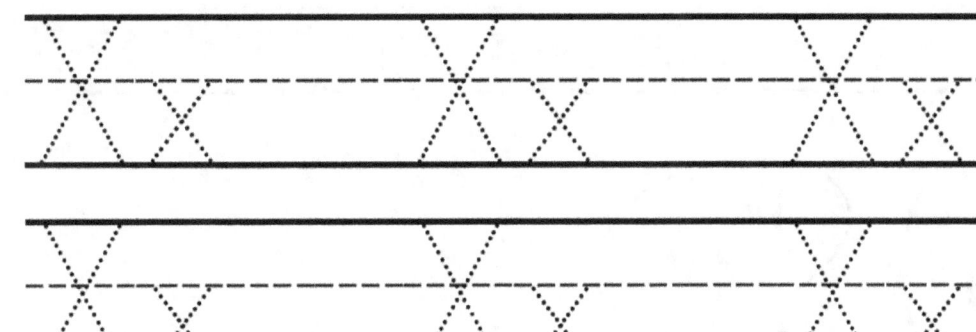

tuttlenfriendsmedia.com   BEEZUS BEE'S Letter Tracing coloring Worksheets   © 2024 Tuttle N Friends media LLC

Can you write the letter below?

Yay!

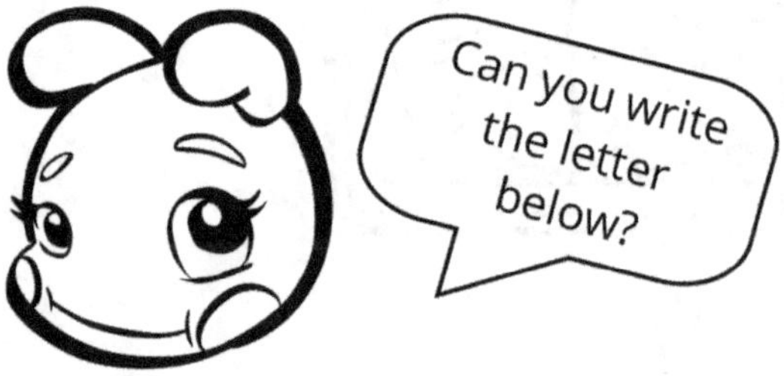

© 2024 Tuttle N Friends media LLC

Name: _____

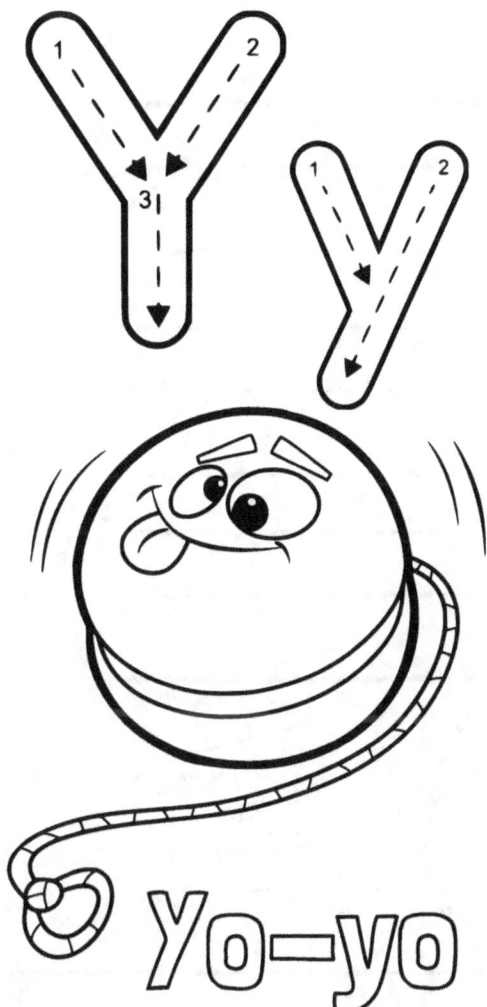

yo-yo

Yak

A B C D E F G H I J K L M N O P Q R S T U V W X **Y** Z

Can you trace these letters?

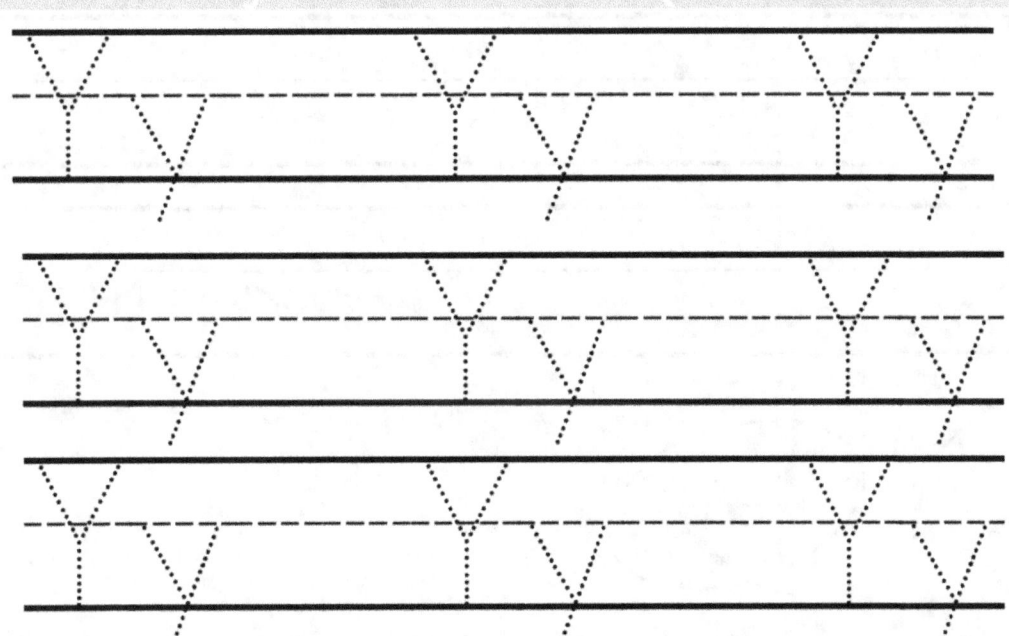

tuttlenfriendsmedia.com

BEEZUS BEE'S Letter Tracing Coloring Worksheets

© 2024 Tuttle N Friends media LLC

Can you write the letter below?

Yay!

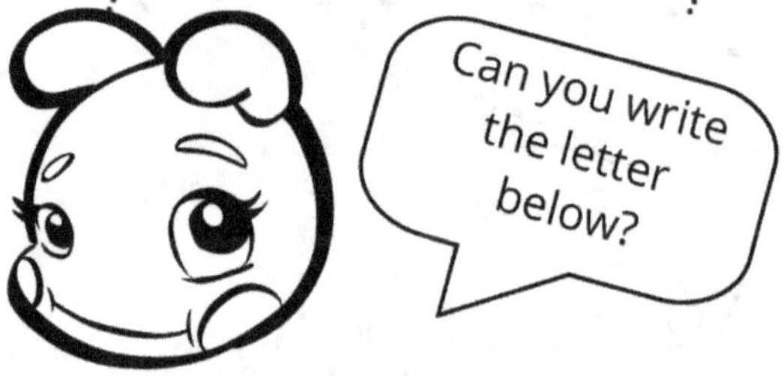

© 2024 Tuttle N Friends media LLC

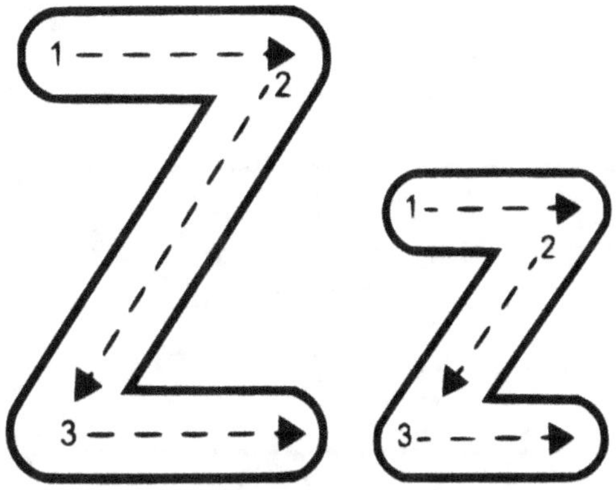

Name: _____

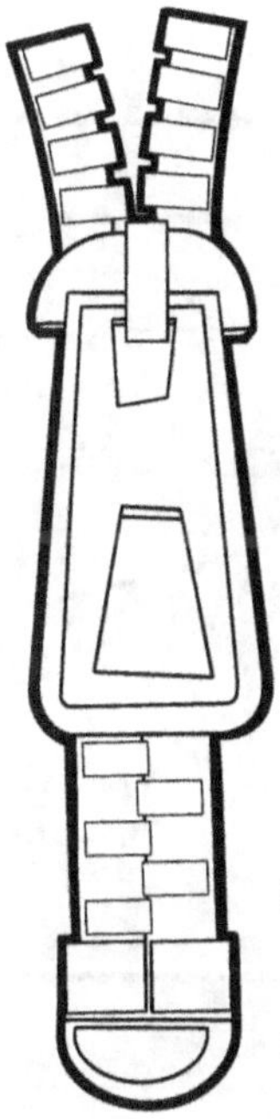

Z z

Zipper

Zebra

A B C D E F G H I J K L M N O P Q R S T U V W X Y Z

Can you trace these letters?

tuttlenfriendsmedia.com
BEEZUS BEE'S Letter Tracing Coloring Worksheets
© 2024 Tuttle N Friends media LLC

Can you write the letter below?

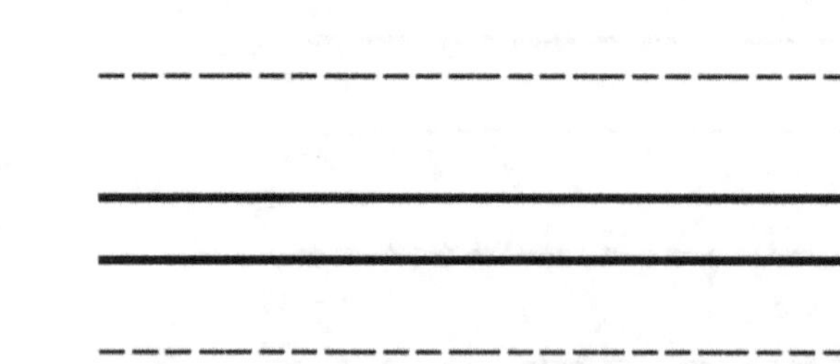

Yay!

© 2024 Tuttle N Friends media LLC

Alphabet Review:

Aa Bb Cc Dd Ee

Ff Gg Hh Ii Jj Kk

Ll Mm Nn Oo Pp

Qq Rr Ss Tt Uu

Vv Ww Xx Yy Zz

BEEZUS BEE'S Letter Tracing Coloring Worksheets   © 2024 Tuttle N Friends media LLC

Name Tracing Practice!

My name is..

write your child's name below:

_____

- - - - - - - - - - - - - - - - - - - -

Can you write your name below?

© 2024 Tuttle N Friends media LLC

© 2024 Tuttle N Friends media LLC

UPPER CASE LETTERS

A B C D E F

G H I J K L

M N O P Q R

S T U V W X

Y Z

BEEZUS BEE'S Letter Tracing Coloring Worksheets

© 2024 Tuttle N Friends media LLC

a b c d e

f g h i j k

l m n o p q

r s t u v w

x y z

BEEZUS BEE'S Letter Tracing Coloring Worksheets

© 2024 Tuttle N Friends media LLC

tuttlenfriendsmedia.com

© 2024 Tuttle N Friends media LLC

This Certificate Is Presented To:

For Completing This Book!

BeezusBee's Handwriting Practice Workbook!

Beezus Bee

_____
Signed By

_____
Date

tuttlenfriendsmedia.com

© 2024 Tuttle N Friends media LLC

Bye Bye!
Thank you for coloring and practicing your letters with me!

♡ BEEZUS

© 2024 Tuttle N Friends media LLC

From the Artist:

Thank you for purchasing this book. I sincerely hope that you and your child enjoyed it. I had a lot of fun creating it and sharing these characters with you. Please consider leaving a review, your feedback is invaluable to me as an independent artist and publisher, and helps me reach more readers.

Thank you!

Gregg Azzopardi

© 2024 Tuttle N Friends media LLC

www.ingramcontent.com/pod-product-compliance
Lightning Source LLC
Chambersburg PA
CBHW081538120626
46550CB00009B/2775